SLAVES ON THE SADDLE

Why it's So Hard for the Black Man to Survive without the White Man

CHRIS LEO

TABLE OF CONTENTS

INTRODUCTION

"There is an evil which I have seen under the sun, *as* it were an error proceeding from the ruler: folly is set in many high places and the rich sit in a low place. I have seen slaves on horses, and princes walking on foot like slaves" – Ecclesiastes 10:5-7 Revised Standard Version

It is said that in the land of the blind one-eyed man is king. This unfortunate position seems however generally accepted in the world today. Why? This is simply because one-eyed man has a leverage; an advantage over the men who are blind, thanks to his one-seeing eye. That is only fair considering the scenario around the world today. His seemingly privileged position makes him boss over others.
But if in the land of the one-eyed men, a blind man is king, then there is a big problem. The problem will be more chaotic, corrosive and catastrophic if a blind man rules over men with 2020 vision. Unfortunately, this later analogy is the situation and stark reality in most lands today especially in our Africa.

This ugly situation is the major contributor to agitations and reasons for constant eruptions and vulcanization of the polity. It is the major cause of bankruptcy and backwardness of Africa's economy, and by extension, the world economy. And until this poor and unfortunate arrangement is cardinally, conscientiously and carefully addressed and altered to the original order, we will continue to have frictions and unnecessary clashes of interests in this God-blessed continent.

In this book, Slaves on the Saddle, I have pointed out who a slave is, the position of a slave, the mentality of a slave and the unfortunate twist that has truncated the system and denied it of ensuring a just and righteous order. I have also discussed the failure of the princes in taking charge, which eventually results in the unfortunate but consequential somersault of positions, and how they can keep their seats from being hijacked any longer.

You will also discover in this book what the saddle is originally made for – its design and designation such that abuse can be eliminated or drastically reduced as the case may be. I did not fail to highlight the need for fairness – to strike a balance in an already lopsided and imbalanced entity. And as my custom is, the last chapter has been dedicated to x-ray the shots as I see them. These last pages encapsulate my musings about this whole quandary and quagmire that seemed to have trapped the world in not a few uncertainties.

For the world to live a harmonious life, the leadership-followership equation must be well-adjusted and balanced knowing that both the slave and the slave-driver come under the authority of the Almighty God who is the Creator of them both, and the Ultimate Designer of the saddle. Otherwise, slaves will continue to rule while the princes live in ruins. A sad state that we must urgently address!

Chris Leo
August 2017

Chapter One

THE SLAVE

According to dictionary definition, a slave is a person owned in law by another. He is a servant without personal freedom, completely in the control of another person. He is one who must obey the one who is in control of him. Now, if we take that definition hook, line and sinker, it will preach a slightly different message from what this book seeks to preach. It will also not be fair enough to address the major characters who we wish to address here by extremely following the terms or definition as given above.

To tag them as people owned in law and without personal freedom would be an aberration – a deviation from truth and moral rectitude. This is so in considering the position of influence destiny placed has them and what divine mandate has bestowed on them.

Moreover, the Word of God in Proverbs 22:2 says, "The rich and the poor meet together; the LORD is the maker of them all".

Suffice it to say that the slave and the owner or slave driver meet together, both come under the authority of God. Therefore, I will try to take from the dictionary definition the lines or idea that apparently fits into our argument and add to it from my perspective. Doing this will help me to communicate much precisely the crux of my message to you.

The dictionary is not the only book that gives or has given a definition of the word "slave". Before even the emergence or arrival of the English Dictionary, God has given us great insight into who a slave is. Bible history has recorded about slavery and slaves centuries before the English dictionary or encyclopedia came to light. As a minister of God and a Bible student and enthusiast, I strongly believe that God knows better than any dictionary and their authors. So, for the Holy Bible to record about slaves is an indication and confirmation that God knows who slaves really are and what their place or position in the society should be.

<u>**Slave Identity**</u>

A slave is a person who is under the control or supervision of another who he works to satisfy. He takes instructions, orders and commands from him and carries them out as expected. He waits on his master for instructions, ready to run errands and do the work well. A slave is a servant who must serve for the comfort of his master, for there lies his own fulfilment. If he must be treated well and cared for and honored, he must therefore do his work well.

A slave is either bought, inherited or hired. Some slaves give themselves up to be slaves to serve in order to earn a living. Some volunteer to render service to their masters. In this book, we shall look at those who give themselves up to serve the people of their communities, constituencies, or countries in various capacities. Are they slaves or masters? We will see right here.

And since slaves are equally servants these people are either civil servants, public servants or private servants who are either elected, appointed or who volunteer to serve their people via any constitutional means. We shall also narrow it down to our community, constituency, and country. And as it comes to us, we may broaden it beyond our borders.

Since we have established that slaves are owned or bought or even hired for a while to do some service, we shall proceed to look at how to identify them and their services. But before we go in that direction, let us look at something that is of profound importance to this book. We have stated that slaves are equally servants since all they do is to render service and run errands as assigned to them by their masters. But what is the position of a slave?

<u>Slave Position</u>

It is worthy of note here the fact that a slave is not a noble. That is, he is not born of noble "blood". In the times of old, people who were usually used as slaves were ordinary people who were either bought from the slave market or conquered in war. However, most slaves were people of ordinary backgrounds who had no royal connection and thus, no reputation as such. This makes a slave to be a lower-class citizen. If he is gotten as spoils of war or a captive, he is given no kind treatment except and until he proves himself worthy of good treatment and honor through his service.

Generally, a slave is considered a poor, wretched, pitiable and miserable fellow who lives at the mercy of his master. His position in the family, community or country is often despised and hardly given good attention. The class of a slave in a community makes him a potential scape goat or sacrificial lamb. It places him in a state of never-being listened to such that he is at risk of being victimized without getting respite or justice.

No one really looks the way of a slave because he is often considered as "down there". The only remedy for this slave is to become a valuable asset to his master. If he proves himself a worthy vessel through hard work and good character, he may earn the mercy and kindness of his master who might begin to treat him with dignity and honor. But for the average slave, he is confined to that relegated position of lowliness, servitude and slavery for the rest of his life.

In reality, that is the position of a slave. It is so despicably so that President Solomon in his writing about it in Ecclesiastes lamented having such a person rule over the nobles. We do not want to stress so much on the identity or position of a slave so that we can look at a more essential highlight for which this book is much concerned. We shall now discuss the last two issues in this first chapter which are more salient than the already discussed.

Slave Mentality

Mind-set is a key in determining how people or a person behaves or conducts himself. This is a set of processes that bother on ones values, tastes, desires, and projections that affect his principles, philosophies and programming. One of the marks or pronounced features of a slave is his mentality. The way he thinks, reasons, views things and moves is usually short of standard. His views are usually narrow, his reasoning too shallow, and his sight quite myopic such that he comes behind in almost every area of life.

In fact, what makes a man a real slave is not his lack of noble or royal blood. It is not his relegated position which is a result of who he really is. It is also not the tribe or ethnic extraction he hails from. It is basically his mind-set or mentality. And this is what we want to major on in the remaining pages of this chapter and most part of this book.

Let me once again reiterate that the central message of this book is to convey how men and women of poor mentality and warped mind-set are holding sway in the community to the detriment of all – people and processes. I am sometimes bewildered by their sudden rise to power and authority in the land. I mean, how they manage to climb the ladder, nay, fly into positions of influence and getting past the nobles of the land leaves me in shock and wonder.

I had tried to calculate the geometry but honestly, the equations do not seem to balance out. For a long time, I placed a strong demand on my brains in constant search and study on intellectual materials to decipher why it has been so, but all my efforts did not amount to much in comparison to the amount of effort put in. Not until recently, as I studied the Holy Bible after writing my thought-provoking series "The Errors of Our Heroes Past" that God began to unveil and reveal things to me.

If we take a look at our communities, constituencies, and our beloved countries especially in the African continent, we will discover that the major problem setting us back is poor mentality. We have allowed certain abnormalities in our midst for too long that they become traditions. An Igbo adage says that when an abominable act is allowed for too long in the community, it metamorphoses into a tradition.

Sincerely, it is not because we are Blacks that it seems like fortune hardly smiles on us. It is not because we live in the Tropics that development seem slow. No! It is not because we live in Africa, this slice of the Earth planet that make people from other parts of the world to despise and deride us. Not at all. It is because of our mentality! Poor mind-set and mentality are our biggest undoing!

Now, if you ask me why the Whites (Europe and America) succeeded in making our fore-fathers slaves, it was because of our ancestors' poor mentality. One becomes a slave to what or who he allows to rule over him. One may argue that the Whites forced our ancestors into slavery with their sophisticated arms and ammunition. That may be apparently true if we view it from one angle. But looking at it holistically, our ancestors had brains – same brains God gave the Whites, but what did they use their "intelligent" brains and minds to do?

The Whites used theirs to advance the core essentials of life by designing and manufacturing tools and technology to rule their world. Our ancestors in Africa used theirs to grab more lands, more wives, and more black power that cannot match the technology of the Whites. It all boils down to what they saw or reasoned as important and essential to their existence.

When a people do not think ahead, they do not see ahead, and when they cannot see ahead, they cannot move ahead. That is to say, you think ahead to see ahead and then to move ahead! All about mentality! I could dedicate a whole book on this later point.

A CASE STUDY

This case study is taken from the fourth book of the Holy Bible, which is, Numbers 13: 1-30. The people of Israel (of Bible times) were slaves and bondmen in Egypt for more than four centuries. God Almighty sent Moses to bring them out. Now, He was taking them through some phases that were intended to remove the slave stigma from them.

At a time, Moses, as commanded by God, sent out men to spy or check out the Promised Land where it was recorded that milk and honey flowed in abundance. Moses did not choose ordinary men. He did not appoint or select men of no reputation for the task. God had told him to appoint leaders from each tribe – men of noble standing in the country – and assigned them the duty. They were to do a thorough feasibility of the land of the Amorites – the Canaan land; the Promised Land – a land of abundance of natural resources.

Just like Africa where nature itself resides, resources flow, and greener pastures are found in abundance from North to South, East to West. As God instructed Moses to appoint men, so Africa has men too – all leaders in their own right. Leaders who have a singular job description – to search out the land, but who must report back their findings.

Their findings as would be contained in their report should include the nature of the land – what it is like; the people of the land – weak or strong, many or few;

the security situation of the land – whether porous or fortified, and the economy of the same place. The state of the economy has to be ascertained whether rich or poor, stable or fluctuating, and whether it supports businesses or not.

They have to look at the natural resources in the land too – whether exportable or just for local consumption. The last instruction was for them to produce evidence of the fruitfulness of the land. Now, the question is: Is such a mission as this impossible? My answer would be No if you asked me. That is a task for leaders.

In Nigeria and Africa, we have a problem. Yes, we have leaders who have received same mandate to explore and exploit in rewarding terms the vast opportunities that litter our lands. We have the presidency with their cabinet of ministers. We have the national and state assemblies with their standing and ad hoc committees. We also have the judiciary with their special panels of enquiry and jury.

From one regime to another, from one administration to another, these people have been there – appointed, elected or even selected to function in various capacities. Their assignments have been severally spelt out even in simple formats and terms. A layman can understand the processes, procedures and protocols, yet these our leaders have continued over the years with little or nothing to show for it.

When they were appointed, elected or selected to do the job, they were extremely happy. They doff their hats for the people whose contributions validated their appointment or election. They usually celebrate the moment, giving praise to the people who support them in attaining the prestigious position so to speak. But along the line, in the line of duty; on the field of assignment, things go wrong. They return with a report. And what is their report? In summary: The mission is impossible! Aha! It cannot be done!

Look at the men, nay, leaders Moses sent out to scout their new country-home. The Bible said that they brought an evil report which threw the entire nation into serious mourning as if God was dead. They said, *"We came to the land to which you sent us; it flows with milk and honey, and this is its fruit. Yet the people who dwell in the land are strong and the cities are fortified and very large; and besides, we saw the descendants of Anak there. The Amalekites dwell in the land of the Negeb; the Hittites, the Jebusites and the Amorites dwell in the hill country: and the Canaanites dwell by the sea, and along the Jordan."* (Vss. 27-29)

Now if you dissect the report, they did part of the assignment well. They described the land – it was fruitful. They confirmed the resources there – milk and honey flowed in it. They also described the kinds of people in the country – the Amalekites in the Negeb, that is, the south; the Hittites, the Jebusites and the Amorites in the hill country, that is, the north; and the Canaanites who dwell by the sea, that is, the coastline. Good job!

They also captured another set of people in their report which they did not mention their locality or region in the country. The descendants of Anak – they were giants. Probably, this last set filled the country of Canaan and that might be the reason their exact dwelling region was not mentioned in the report.

Now let us dissect further and bring it home. I will use Nigeria as the 'giant' of Africa to analogize my points. It is like saying, 'We came to the country and found the Yorubas and Ijaws in the South; the Hausas, the Fulanis, and the Tivs in the North; the Igbos, the Ibibios and their neighbors in the Niger Delta.

Then, we also saw some terrorists – Boko Haram, Herdsmen, Kidnappers, Ritual killers – in the land. However, the resources are good. See the crude oil, palm oil, cocoa, tin ore, groundnut, and there are still a variety of others we could not bring along". Then, what is next? Let us paint the picture a bit further and clearer.

On the floor of the National or State Assembly, Senator Caleb (put any Senator or lawmaker's name there if you like) representing Judah Senatorial Zone or Constituency as the case may be, raised his hand, and made a very compulsory interruption – a point of order.

Perhaps, he had said, 'Mr. Speaker and fellow distinguished lawmakers, let us mobilize our people from all our constituencies and begin to occupy the land. We are able to make this country a paradise in the world. The terrorists are no match for our military and high-spirited citizens.' But usually and disappointingly too, you would hear, 'Those in favor say 'I', and those against say, 'Nay'. The 'Nays' have it. And the gavel nails it home.

<u>'The Majority Carries the Vote'</u>

History confirmed this sad development with the following lines: "Then the men who had gone up with him (Caleb) said, "We are not able to go up against the people; for they are stronger than we," saying, "The land, through which we have gone to spy it out, is a land that devours its inhabitants; and all the people that we saw in it are men of great stature. And there we saw the Nephilim (the sons of Anak, who came from the Nephilim); and we seemed to ourselves like grasshoppers, and so we seemed to them" (vs. 31-33). All of a sudden, there was commotion and chaos in the house. Just look at that! Slaves!

If these men were upstarts, novices, and ordinary men in the country, one could excuse their blatant low appraisal of themselves and treat their report with a jaunty wave of the hand. But they were clan heads, leaders of the people who were being looked unto and expected to have strong spine for shouldering tough responsibilities. But no way!

A flashback to their profile according to the Message Bible reveals: "…Send one man from each ancestral tribe, each one a tried-and-true leader in the tribe. So Moses sent them off…All of them were leaders in Israel…" (Vs. 2-3). Does this not paint a familiar and similar picture of the Nigerian and African dilemma?

Here, we have leaders – presidents, governors, lawmakers, high court judges, managing directors, directors-general, senior managers, traditional rulers, political party chieftains and the likes. All these people often claim to be tried, true and trusted to handle national and state problems.

During elections, they are always in high spirits campaigning and trumpeting their self-acclaimed profiles for the various offices they wish to be elected into. They woo the people, that is, the nobles, with their verbosity and often memorized rhetoric. Eventually, they are elected, selected or appointed as it applies.

But soon after, they encounter challenges which are only natural to the task. What next? The blame game begins. They shift their incompetence to the enormity of the task: *"...it's a land that swallows people whole"*. If that is not enough, they push it to the opposition thus: *"Everybody we saw was huge and they looked down on us as if we were grasshoppers"*. But the truth is hidden in themselves, which of course they do not seem to hide for long. Their problem is poor mind-set: *"Alongside them we felt like grasshoppers"*. Low self-esteem! Poor mentality! Slaves!!!

Mentality Configuration

Mind-set is a set of processes that go on in the mind. Mentality is the ability or inability of the mind or mental faculty to manage these sets of processes well. The following can be deduced from the report of those leaders:

Fear: They love their lives so much, but not unto death. This is why our leaders in Africa selfishly inserted the immunity clause in our constitution. They do not want to be touched so they turned themselves into sacred cows and looked for others to make the scape-goats. They however forgot that cows, no matter how sacred, remain lower animals compared to human beings.

This fear of becoming victims in facing challenges that confront their country has kept them from making strong attempts to solve problems. They go back and forth debating issues for a whole tenure only to realize that another election time beckons when they do not expect any "sane" citizen to bother them with national, state or local government issues.

Every other problem of the people is tossed aside until after a new government is elected or the incumbent returns to power. Then, they may either consider the problems on ground or keep them on the shelf and start all over.

Low Self-Esteem: Imagine how they rated themselves: *"Alongside them we felt like grasshoppers."* These are leaders who claim to be tested and trusted, thus qualified for the task of leading the nation. They immediately forget that they are leaders of the people. If they as leaders feel like grasshoppers in the eyes of their opponents or alongside the opposition, how would the people they are leading then feel?

If our national assemblies, presidency, or judiciary cannot see themselves as leaders who can stand up and be counted, what do they expect from ordinary citizens of country and continent?

A little threat in the guise of diplomacy by foreign nations makes some of our leaders squirm in their seats as if heaven would fall. And you see them running from this blessed land to those nations bowing down and begging for support in the name of loans and aid.

One of the things engrained in the mentality of a slave is low self-esteem. This trait in him results in poor self-assessment. He does not know his real worth, and even when he is made to know it, he does not seem to appreciate it.

Incompetence: This was the first response of those leaders that Moses sent out. They confessed: *"We be not able to go up against the people; for they are stronger than we."* Slaves! Then, why did you accept the office? Why did you jump into the wagon when the call "Who will go for us?" was made?

Why did you, Mr. President, Honorable Lawmaker, Mr. Governor, Mr. Chairman, etc., accept to run for that office when you knew that the task of leading the people is not for incompetent folks? There is always a problem with a typical Nigerian and by extension, an African. They love the title more than the task! They confuse feeling with reality. You hear one say, 'I feel God is leading me to be the president or governor or chairman of a local council...' They feel it, not really know it. And that is why we are where we are as a people.

In the build-up to the 2015 general elections in Nigeria, the All Progressives Congress, that is, the main opposition political party which is a coalition of three other political fronts, came up with what they christened The Change Mantra. With bunches of native broom sticks, they promised to sweep away corruption, perversion, and all the likes, and change the status quo as it were.

The major political characters of the party took turns to demonstrate their readiness by pledging and promising a change that would be visible even to a blind man. That was 2015, and this is 2017. We are yet to see their magic wand or miracle rod in action.

One of them was quoted as saying, **"A serious government will fix power in six months"** (November 12th, 2014). He was quoted as having earlier said: **"The only way to have stable electricity is to vote out PDP"** (July 12th, 2014 The Nation Newspapers). Yet, it took six months after they won the elections in March 2015 to announce the cabinet of ministers that would "fix" the light and other palaver. Gross incompetence! Let us move on, please.

<u>Slave Activity</u>

Someone once told me that slaves beg, but kings brag. How true! Actions, they say, speak louder than voice. People are easily known and classified by what they do, more often than what they say. Jesus Christ said, ***"By their fruits, you shall know them"***. I love The Living Bible rendering of that scripture: ***"Yes, the way to identify a tree or a person is by the kind of fruit produced."*** Just to buttress it with a quote by President Solomon Jedidah David of Israel,

"Fools on the road have no sense of direction. The way they walk tells the story: 'There goes the fool again'". (Ecclesiastes 10:5 TM). An African adage says that it is from childhood that you know a child that would end a debtor at old age.

Let me tell you a funny true life story. My late grandmother, my uncle and my father all shared this story with us in the family. Everyone in town at that time probably knew about it. A certain woman was at the town's market one evening when her church catechist rode his bicycle past her shop without stopping over for the usual greetings. So this woman concluded, 'If the Catechist could not stop over to greet me as usual, it then means my son has failed the catechism examinations.' Was she right after all? Of course, she was!

Going back to our case study again, I mean, the Israel of old, one could see the damage that over 400 years of slavery in Egypt did to the people. Every step of the way to possess their new homeland after crossing the Red Sea was filled with clamor, rancor, bickering, murmurs, and rhetorical debates and dumbfounding drama. It was either they complained of lack of water, food or they wanted to return to slavery in

Egypt. What a very disappointing way to celebrate their independence! They were never grateful for their freedom. Fairly, they did so only when the going was smooth and good. Slaves!

Nigeria and many other African countries crossed the red sea of colonization in 1960. Some people who presented themselves as leaders or who were hand-picked as leaders received the mandate to map out ways to settle and spread – going forward.

The task was not that simple, but was do-able. The mission was not heck-free, but not impossible. The journey began with good prospects as it were, but soon some of those saddled with that responsibility lost focus and veered into a white-goose chase for self-announcement, self-dependence, and self-aggrandizement. Then, anarchy loomed.

By their ignoble activities and actions, the entire land was thrown into another dimension of slavery. It appeared their once slave nature boomeranged and they went back to what got them into slavery from the beginning.

Now, ask yourself: How do people become slaves? A wise leader like Solomon has ready answers to that one question.

"The rich ruleth over the poor, and the borrower is servant (slave) *to the lender"* (Proverbs 22:7). One of the activities of slaves is **borrowing**. In fact, this is one of the things that makes a free man to become a slave. He hardly thinks of a way to pay bills other than to borrow. A slave even borrows from those beneath him. He does this because he has a low self-esteem and so incompetent to create other sources of revenue for himself, his family and the country.

Recently, the world financial and money managers, IMF, revealed that Nigeria would not be able to sustain her borrowing capacity to maintain debts. So, they advised against continuous borrowing with the evident bleak economy and inflation in the country.

But the minister of finance and her employers – the federal government would not listen to that sound, timely caution. Why? They do not see any other noble way to fund the budget. Too bad! Wisest President Solomon reveals: *"Just as the rich rule the poor, so the borrower is servant to the lender"* (TLB).

If I should paraphrase it, I would say, 'Just as the rich has power over the poor, the borrower is slave to the lender.'

But how can a slave survive without borrowing? It is already in him so he will find it difficult, if not impossible to change. Just as a slave thinks he has no capacity and capability to face the economic, political and social challenges confronting him and solve them, he does not see a way out of financial bottle-necks except by borrowing.

By this, he throws the whole country into undeserving slavery. Eugene Peterson in his Message Bible translation cautions: *"...so don't borrow and put yourself under their power"*. But will these leaders listen? No! Why? Your guess could be as good as my answer.

What other activity does a slave engage in? It is begging. **Slaves beg** to feed and survive. If they happen to be state leaders or national leaders, they beg to fund their state and national budgets. If they happen to be employers of labor, they beg to pay salaries of their workers. They even beg them to bear with them over their inability, nay, unwillingness to pay them their due wages. Ha! What embarrassment!

Is it because they truly cannot pay their workers? Is it because they do not have enough to fund their budgets? No sir! No ma! You know, beggars may have more than enough to cater for their needs, but will still beg for alms or for aid. If he is an individual, he will beg for alms which often come as crumbs. If he is a state governor, he will beg the president and his executive council for aid which may come as bailout funds to pay workers' salaries.

If a company, they will beg investors or even the public for bailout through some media paparazzi in the guise of promotions. Why do they beg? It is because they believe that they do not have enough. Why do they not have enough? It is because they waste resources in the time of plenty.

Now ask them what they do with those resources? The answer will shock you. Beggars only wish to become; they do not feel secure about their status whether they have or not. It is in their blood to live like that.

Now back to the question I asked; is it truly because they lack the capacity to settle or pay their bills that leads to their begging from others? The answer lies in the next point – another activity that confirms their slave status.

Slaves Squander. To explain this point, let me refer to the illustration Jesus Christ gave in the Bible book of Luke chapter twelve from verse sixteen. *"A rich man had a fertile farm that produced fine crops. In fact, his barns were full to overflowing – he couldn't get everything in. he thought about his problem, and finally exclaimed, 'I know – I'll tear down my barns and build bigger ones! Then I'll have room enough. And I'll sit back and say to myself, "Friend, you have enough stored away for years to come. Now take it easy! Wine, women, and song for you."*

Did you see that? Let us see how this rich man acted as a slave. We will not look at the bumper harvest – the internally generated revenue, profit after tax, monthly allocation, constituency allowance, etc. But we will look at his reaction or response to the arrival of plenty harvest. This is where his attitude and lifestyle of wantonness are brazenly revealed.

"...he couldn't get everything in". Slaves lack capacity. Yes, they lack the capacity to get all revenues in. Whether it is community, constituency, state or federal revenues – they never seem to have the ability to bring them in.

This is one of the numerous plagues ravaging our Africa. We are divinely blessed with natural and human resources. We have the human brains to exploit all we have been generously given. But our problem is the crop of people who occupy the various decision-making positions in the country. They have not lived up to expectation in this regard.

Their policies and programs have not supported the mechanism for exploiting these overflowing resources for economic growth and national development. And this is the biggest and worst nightmare confronting and terrifying us as a continent.

You know, when a servant who is used to manage his master's wealth in the millions is put in charge of billions which only nobles can manage effectively and efficiently well, tendencies are that he will not know how to handle the level. Worse still, he might not have the skills to harness all available resources. This is the problem most of our leaders are actually having. They do not know how to get all in. So they think it is their problem.

"He thought about his problem..." Most leaders do not see natural challenges in their domain as everybody's challenge. They see it as their problems. It is always about them. This is what slave mentality does to people. So instead of employing the expertise of qualified personnel in discussing and discerning the right approach and strategies to solving the problems, they see themselves as the only messiah.

The slave mentality in them will not let them seek solutions from others. This is because they do not trust others to handle issues of national or state concerns. That is the same spirit that is pushing some politicians around here. The *'I, me and myself'* syndrome. Look at that illustration again, and you will see the **'I's Have It'** syndrome. It did not start today, folks.

Since he is the only one soliloquizing on the issue, an issue that should concern all stakeholders; issue that should be properly addressed for the benefit of all;

he sees it as 'his problem'. And what does his warped, myopic mind tell him to do? Please, read with me.

'I know – I'll tear down my barns...' Slaves! They love to dismantle existing structures, not to redesign and restructure them. They love to destroy existing policies, not to modify them. They like to proscribe existing agencies and not revitalize them. They like to put their national projects on concession after years of wasting enormous resources on them, instead of putting them in the hands of qualified countrymen and women to efficiently manage them.

Why do they do these? Because the existing policies, structures and agencies pose serious threat to their selfish ambitions and hidden agendas. If they meet any working concept on ground when they assume office, they do all in their tiny power to frustrate it so as to initiate their own, name it after them and make humongous cash from it. Slaves!

They always feel threatened by successful ideas as long as those ideas do not come from them nor support their unpatriotic bigotry. That is what some call small-mindedness. No one else merits the honor or credit except them.

In tearing down existing structures, they use state funds to hire foreign hands and machines. In the process, huge amounts that would have been channeled into infrastructural projects and human capital development to benefit the common man are wasted.

Slaves love to squander. Why? Many reasons pop up in my mind, but one of them appeals most to me. They feel that their masters used them to gather the wealth which is now in their custody. So they have that entitlement mentality; that they should enjoy now they are in charge. And in building back the torn projects, oh, they squander more and more.

When you calculate the volume of waste by these people in Nigeria and Africa, you would weep for the land. No wonder President Solomon lamented, ***"Woe is the land whose king*** (president, leader, etc.) ***is but a child!"*** (Ecclesiastes 10:16, emphasis mine). I should put it this way, "Woe is the country whose president is a slave!"

Thank God he did not mention any king's name, but I believe Solomon must have seen kings in his time who ruled their countries like children. But by the wisdom of God, he was careful not to mention their names. So, I follow in his style – no name-calling. Slaves know themselves; no need to publish their names; that is not what this book seeks to accomplish. I think that is fair enough.

Slaves Store Away For Themselves. Look at that rich man's pathetic story again: *'And I'll sit back and say to myself, 'Friend, you have enough stored away for years to come'*. Slave mentality! Slave activity! Slave attitude! A very sad way to live!

Go outside Africa to other countries like Switzerland, United Arab Emirate, Europe and America, you would discover our sovereign wealth stored away for years by these men and women. Slaves never store their stolen master's wealth in their country because they know it would be easy for their masters to find out. They store it away for themselves and their rather unfortunate progeny so that when they are thrown out, they have something outside to fall back on.

They tell themselves, 'Look, we are slaves, and will not be here forever. Now that we are in charge, let us settle ourselves before our time runs out. These people – our inherited masters – can decide to dispose us after first or second tenure in office and hire other people. We must not end up as errand boys and girls and be mocked by them'. Slaves!

When you listen to musings like this, it reveals the degree of foolishness of a slave. He does not think of storing the stolen wealth in his land because he is foolish and selfish. He is also ignorant of the fact that the countries he runs to store away his stolen wealth also have slaves who could be wise enough to use it and develop their country!

Remember the movie of the thief who stole from the rich to help the poor. Smart white guys! So, our slaves might claim to be patriotic but never come near to the meaning of the word. And if they are compelled to store the loot within our borders, they make sure that it does not yield any turnovers for their masters. That is why we have witnessed as alleged and revealed by anti-graft agencies how these people store theirs away in soak-away pits and empty towers.

Jesus gave another illustration worthy of note. Matthew 25:14-30. The master gave three of his servants the opportunity to serve by trading with his money. Two of them doubled their master's money while the third servant stored his away in a napkin – no profit made on it! What was his reason?

Since the profit would not be his, neither should his master have it. He has a slave mind-set. That is the same case with so many leaders in our dear land. They store away wealth in foreign lands for themselves so that the common man in the country would not benefit from it. They build companies and factories in foreign lands so that the people here do not have jobs and earn and live prosperous lives.

They build refineries in foreign lands and make sure the ones in their country do not work. This is all in a bid to make the people poor so they could worship them. They take our crude to foreign lands, refine them in their refineries and those of their partners in slavery, and bring in the products only to sell to us at outrageous amounts. Slaves!

But thank God for Jesus as he ended that illustration with this: *"Cast the unprofitable servant* (turned slave) *into outer darkness, where there is wailing and gnashing of teeth."* Our God shall make all those who have swallowed our collective wealth to vomit them some day!

Slaves Love Pleasure. The last point in looking at the slave activity as contained in the story narrated by Jesus Christ is their penchant for pleasure. That slave rich man told himself, *"Now take it easy! Wine, women and song for you!"* Slaves! Oh, how they love pleasure! They love to embark on endless frivolities at the expense of their soul and the comfort of other country men.

President Solomon lamented, *"Woe to thee, O land, when thy king is a child, and thy princes eat in the morning!"* The man wept for the country where leaders behaved like slaves. Only slaves eat and get drunk in the morning when work has not even been done. Nobles do not love pleasure; they take a break after they have done their noble task. And if they dine and wine, I mean the nobles, it is for renewal of strength to do more work and complete the task.

President Solomon confirms this: *"Happy the land whose king is a nobleman and whose leaders work hard before they feast and drink, and then only to strengthen themselves for the tasks ahead"* (TLB).

Just take a look at most of the leaders in Africa. President Solomon carefully and prophetically captured them in his ecclesiastical treatise. Billions of naira are voted for refreshment for our executives, lawmakers, ministers and ambassadors, even at the backdrop of their seeming redundancy and stark recession in the land. Let them show Nigerians the justification for this stupendous, frivolous and inglorious waste of our collective patrimony and taxpayers' money. None! Obviously and absolutely no justification!

Instead of using the time allotted them to debate on fundamental issues that would benefit the common man, they dwell and debate on issues that majorly concern themselves. What a pity! How could a lawmaker be receiving hardship allowance when the ordinary citizen who is suffering real hardship is left to ruin? This is outrageous abomination! President Solomon cried out in despair and frustration, *"I have seen servants upon horses, and princes walking as servants upon the earth."*

The people suffering hardship are not given any relief; it is the people who are receiving fat salaries, allowances and emoluments that are being further refreshed with hardship allowance. Should we keep quiet about this? Not on your life, sir. God Almighty has commissioned us to speak out, nay, write out and publish it out. And we will not betray our divine mandate. Slaves! They love pleasure at the expense of the perishing souls. It does not matter who they are; their nomenclature does not make any difference as long as they do not care much about the perishing people of this continent. They are slaves!

To buttress the fact and point that one of the roguishly outstanding features of a slave is his love for pleasure, Jesus Christ has this to add: *"And not many days after the younger son gathered all together, and took his journey into a far country, and there wasted his substance with riotous living. And when he had spent all, there arose a mighty famine in that land; and he began to be in want"* (Luke 15:13-14).

For better understanding, read this version: *"A few days later this younger son packed all his belongings and took a trip to a distant land, and there wasted*

all his money on parties and prostitutes..." (TLB).
Slaves! Even though he was a free-born son of his
father, yet he turned himself into a slave, and
squandered all his wealth on parties and prostitutes.
What a prodigal way to live and handle wealth.
Slaves!

To conclude this chapter, I have good news and bad
news for these servants-turned-slaves who in one
way or another find themselves in privileged
positions across the land. First the bad news, then the
good news.

The bad news is contained in another illustration by
Jesus the Christ in Luke 19:22, *"You vile and wicked
slave...If you knew so much about me and how
tough I am, then why didn't you deposit the money
in the bank so that I could at least get some interest
on it?"* (TLB).

He added from Matthew 25:28 thus: *"Take the
money from this man and give it to the man with the
$10,000. For the man who uses well what is given
shall be given more, and he shall have abundance.
But from the man who is unfaithful, even what little
responsibility he has shall be taken from him. And*

throw the useless servant (turned slave) out into outer darkness: there shall be weeping and gnashing of teeth." (TLB)

Sad news – there is always judgement awaiting slaves, especially the lazy, wicked, vile and prodigal slaves. One day, either God alone through cardiac arrest as in some cases in the past or through the people will arrest them and thrust them out. It happened in Egypt, in Tanzania, in Cote D'Ivoire, and in Libya. My country should pray hard else it might happen if these servants do nothing to change the status quo.

Now to good news. Luke 15:17-19, Jesus the Christ narrates, *"When he finally came his senses (meaning he lost his senses earlier), he said to himself, 'At home even hired men have food enough and to spare, and here I am, dying of hunger! I will go home to my father and say, 'Father, I have sinned against both heaven and you, and am no longer worthy of being called your son. Please take me on as a hired man"* (TLB) emphasis mine.

There is yet opportunity for you who have squandered our national wealth. You can still receive pardon from the people of this beautiful continent. Yes, you can still be accepted back as a good man who only lost focus and failed his people.

This young man concluded to return home and plead for forgiveness. He also confessed that he was no longer qualified for the privilege and treatment he once received at home as a son, but rather preferred to be treated as a hired man, that is, a slave. Of course, that was what he turned himself into. But that is not the good news, here it is: *"So he returned home to his father. And while he was still a long distance away, his father saw him coming, and was filled with loving pity and ran and embraced him and kissed him"* (vs. 20).

While it will certainly be so hard for the African people to forgive, welcome home and embrace their leaders who have squandered their national and sovereign wealth if they repent today, it is of utmost importance for the culprits to embrace repentance like the prodigal son.

I know our penchant for seeing looters and embezzlers face the full wrath of the law, but it is important we note that this is the first reaction of the people – and they have the right to. However, whether the people who have been downtrodden choose to forgive or not, those who have been prodigal with the wealth of the nation should explore the leeway of repentance and hope they are forgiven and welcomed back with embrace.

After all, if they would feel bad when not forgiven, then they should also have avoided being wasteful with what belongs to their people. How I pray that regardless of whether these slaves are pardoned or not, the people whose right it is to have the throne should do the needful and keep their saddle from being maliciously hijacked.

[48]

Chapter Two

THE SLAVE DRIVERS

Every slave has a driver; someone that owns him or controls him. An African adage says that even a land is being owned by someone. There is no land that is No-Man's-Land! Psalm 24 say, *"The earth is the Lord's and the fullness thereof; the lands, and the inhabitants therein."* So, slaves are being driven or controlled by some people who we shall refer to as slave drivers.

It is a known fact that actions and reactions are equal but opposite as propounded by Sir Isaac Newton – the father of physics. Every reaction is a direct or indirect response to an action. It may be directly proportional or indirectly proportional to the action.

In this chapter, we shall not only see who the slave drivers are in the context of this writing, but we shall see the method of the slave drivers that contrast their endowed status. We shall look at the dilemma confronting these sets of people such that gives the slaves the impetus to take over the saddle.

Identity of a Slave Driver

Since we are not treating or designating slaves in this book as people owned, we shall also look at slave drivers as those who do not own the slaves but in a way determine their performance. Let us look at them as those who hire the slaves for service. Since a slave is one who is hired or bought with a price to render a service, the slave driver is a beneficiary of the service. While the slave renders the service, the slave driver enjoys the service.

Therefore, the slave driver is the one who by natural endowment or any other arrangement is entitled to receive the services of the slave in total submission, loyalty under the climate or ceiling of fairness and cordiality. This means that the slave driver enjoys the expected blessings and benefits in an atmosphere of harmonious relationship with the slave.

Now, let us narrow the identity of the slave driver to three specifics. They are **noblemen**. They are **naturally endowed** with wealth. But most of them are unfortunately **naïve** about issues. Basically, these are the points I would like to treat as striking features of our contextual slave drivers.

NOBLEMEN: A nobleman is a man of noble rank, title or status. He could be a patrician or peer whose ranks range from a baron to a king or to an emperor. He is a free-born son of the land, not someone who becomes a citizen by some artificial or unnatural means.

In our usual term, he is the son of the soil who should enjoy all the wealth of his community and country. A nobleman is not a hireling; he is an overseer of the land and its wealth and resources. There are some outstanding marks or features of a nobleman. They are actually what makes him a man of great standing and noble worth in the society.

Below are some of the features of a noble man:

a. **Integrity** – A nobleman is a man of high degree of integrity. By this, we mean that he is honest, truthful, accountable, faithful, trustworthy, dependable, etc. He is complete, lacking nothing.

b. **Good Name and Reputation** – He is a man that has a good name in the society. *"There was a man in the land of Uz, whose name was Job..."* (Job 1:1

RSV). God gave the record of the man and wrote down his name as a good name.

What makes a name good is as listed in the next line: *'...and that man was blameless, and upright, one who feared God, and turned away from evil.'* These attributes made the name, Job, a name to associate and identify with. Before ever mentioning his wealth of posterity and prosperity, estates and economy, these virtues were first captured about him. These are what make a man truly noble. *"...one that feared God..."* was his reputation and if we move further to chapter twenty-nine of the same Book of Job, we will see more.

c. **Prudence** – Another mark or feature of a nobleman is his ability to be prudent in matters. Sir Matthew Hale said, **"Prudence is principally in actions to be done, and due means, order, seasons, and method of doing or not doing"** (Prose Quotations from Socrates to Marcaulay, J.B. Lippincott Pg. 597, by Samuel Austin Allibone 1876).

This special attribute showcases wisdom in managing provisions and resources especially in way of caution to avoid frivolity, and embracing frugality. So, we can say that a nobleman is not one who squanders wealth or embezzles his nation's funds and treasury. He is not a thief or executive robber who uses pen and privileged position in the land to rob his country blind. Only a slave does that. So, a nobleman, a slave driver is a good manager of resources whether they are natural or human resources.

d. **Peaceful** – A nobleman is a man of peace. He does not encourage violence in the society nor sponsors communal clashes, and later begins to initiate moves to reconcile them.

What we witness today are situations where highly placed individuals who claim to be noblemen pitch communities and neighborhoods against one another. After the damage is done, they begin to arrange press briefings, community town hall meetings and peace talks so that the people would see them as peacemakers. Meanwhile, they are responsible for the breakdown of law and order.

Whenever you see a man – leader or follower – who has no fear of God; who lacks integrity as discussed above, and who is maliciously prodigal with the collective resources of the state or nation; begins to preach peace to warring communities, check again, he might be the sponsor of such conflicts. He is not a man of peace.

In our land today where common herdsmen are carrying arms and ammunitions, invading quiet and peaceful communities and unleashing mayhem on them, probe well, you will find out it is one or more persons of high rank behind them. Unfortunately, they are the first to initiate or call for the setting up of a panel of enquiry or investigation into the matter. Why do they do it? It is so that the rest of the people could see them as peacemakers and peace lovers.

A true peace lover does not wait for conflicts to arise before he begins to preach peace. In fact, to know a peace-loving man, he moves to forestall conflicts by intervening when the trouble is brewing. This is because his ears are always on the ground to hear about those challenges before they erupt in the community. *"Blessed are the peacemakers, for they shall be called the sons of God."*

Justice – A nobleman is a man of equity and justice. Job said, *"When I went out to the gate of the city, when I prepared my seat in the square, the young men saw me and withdrew, and the aged arose and stood; the princes refrained from talking, and laid their hand on their mouth; the voice of the nobles was hushed, and their tongue cleaved to the roof of their mouth. When the ear heard, it called me blessed, and when the eye saw, it approved because I delivered the poor who cried, and the fatherless who had none to help him. The blessings of him who was about to perish came upon me, and I caused the widow's heart to sing for joy. I put on righteousness, and it clothed me; my justice was like a robe and a turban. I was eyes to the blind, and feet to the lame. I was a father to the poor, and I searched out the cause of him whom I did not know. I broke the fangs of the unrighteous, and made him drop his prey from his teeth"* (29:7-17 RSV).

This was why God concluded that there was none like Job on the planet earth.

Fellow Africans, what would people write about you when you are gone from here? Even now, are you a man of justice? A man of justice is a man of noble character.

Anyone who does not love justice will be blacklisted by God. This is the reason Nigeria's judicial system has been in shambles – a total failure! The result then is that no fight against corruption and injustice and impunity ever succeeds. Musician and poet Asaph cried out in the Book of Psalm, *"How long will you [magistrates or judges] judge unjustly and show partially to the wicked? [pause and calmly think of that]! Do justice to the weak (poor) and fatherless, maintain the rights of the afflicted and needy"* (82:2-3 AMP).

Any land where injustice prevails, check again, it is being ruled by people with slave mind-set, not by the noble in character. This is because noblemen do not delight in injustice and will not encourage it among their rank and file. They wear justice like a robe and a turban. Justice is a crown on the head of noblemen. It is a precious crown that cannot fit the head of fools. This is because only fools do not approve of justice for it indicts them.

Fools hide under the temporary and delusive veil of immunity to do injustice and impunity. They have enough stolen funds to shut the mouth of corrupt judges to bury justice just because they find themselves in the saddle at the moment. But God, the Ruler of the Ends of the Earth and Governor among the Nations is about to turn the tables; they shall be called to answer no matter how long it takes.

A nobleman fights for the right of others until justice is served or done. *"For he does not enjoy hurting people or causing them sorrow. If people crush underfoot all the prisoners of the land, if they deprive others of their rights in defiance of the Most High, if they twist justice in the courts – doesn't the Lord see all these things?"* (Lamentations 3:33-36 NLT). God does not approve of injustice and so also a nobleman because he is a man that loves doing the right thing.

NATURALLY WEALTHY: A slave driver is naturally endowed with wealth. His wealth is either inherited, transferred, or acquired by himself. This wealth is one of the major leverages he has over a slave. *"The rich rules over the poor..."* (Proverbs 22:7 NASB).

Abraham in the Bible is an example of a naturally wealthy man. It is recorded: *"Abram took Sarai his wife, and Lot his brother's son, and all their possessions that they had gathered, and the persons [servants] (or slaves) that they had acquired in Haran, and they went forth to go to the land of Canaan..."* (Genesis 12:5 AMP emphasis mine).

This man had slaves and servants who were born and raised in his own house (Genesis 14:14). So in the time of lawful slavery and slave trading, only men like Abraham and his contemporaries were privileged to own slaves. No poor man could afford some prized slaves in that era.

In fact, one of the factors that turns people into slaves is poverty. So the slave driver is a rich nobleman. Not only did they have male and female servants and slaves, they were also blessed with livestock. The slave drivers also have natural resources such as gold mines, coal mines, large farmlands and plantations. Most of the White slave traders from Europe and America that came to Africa had these things where they forced our African ancestors to work and develop for them.

In modern times, in this era of abolished slavery, those who hire the services of others could be described as our slave drivers. However, in the context that I am writing, they are the free-born citizens of the country. They are the original land owners, the oil field owners, plantation owners, and coal and gold mines owners.

They are the indigenes of our ancestral communities who by nature inherited the vast lands and their resources from their ancestors. These are people who should typically own, purchase or transfer slaves as they wish, and thereby control the economy, polity, and the entire spheres of their collective existence.

Their wealth is not artificial. Their wealth is not stolen wealth. In fact, there is nothing for them to steal; no reason for them to steal anything because they are naturally wealthy – they own everything that nature has so generously bequeathed them. If any one of them stole in those days, he would be made to return it or face banishment by their kith and kin. This is because they would be seen as having lost their sense of nobility and assumed to be under the influence of some spell.

These people know their bounds, and would not cross them. They have the law engraved on their hearts and palms, they would not contravene them. They have respect for their customs and traditions which are the pivot on which their collective existence is pitched. In our contemporary time, they are patriotic and loyal to the system they pledge fealty and allegiance to.

They are neither greedy nor desire the dainties or the vanities that present themselves in the guise of privilege of positions or office. They see their privileged position as a divine stool on which they sit to execute a divine mandate and to manage both the slaves, not really to drive them, and the vast natural resources that nature has placed at their disposal and discretion.

Let us not get this all mixed up: These people did not become masters because they coveted the office. God through the natural process of creation, procreation and order bequeathed it upon them. Their wealth does not necessarily measure in cash nor their tangible assets as a result of hard-work; it came to them by entitlement as free-born. This is the major reason for their contentment. Because all things are theirs, they do not grapple for anything. No nobleman runs after the forbidden, only slaves do!

Finally, the wealth of the noblemen inspires them to tend to manage their slaves rather than milk them dry. They take pleasure and pride in their prized slaves. A prized slave here is one who maintains his place in his master's employ without the ungodly desire for the forbidden. We will discuss more on this in subsequent pages.

NAÏVE: The first two attributes of a slave driver so far discussed are quite different in my perspective from this third one. We have established that a slave driver in the context of this writing is both a noble and naturally wealthy man. But this third point or feature appears distinct from them, and somehow incompatible. Howbeit, we will take it from the angle that will communicate our perspective to prevent any form of mix-up.

The word "naïve" from the Latin "nativus" and French "naïve" means to lack worldly experience, wisdom or judgement. Naivety produces lack of sophistication in a person. Such a person becomes gullible or imprudent. Because of this, he often expresses the willingness to believe in someone even at the backdrop of lack of reasonable proof. This attribute is one major undoing of our naturally wealthy nobleman who is our typical slave driver in this context.

Let us make it plainer. The character of nobility in him fills his heart with empathy for his slaves or servants. In the process of expressing this virtue in his relationship with the servants, he opens himself up to deception. His tender-heartedness which makes him more a slave supervisor than a slave driver often exposes his hidden weakness, which in turn, leaves him gullible and vulnerable too. This scenario presents his servants with the opportunity to deceive him.

Being naïve, from my perspective, does not really translate to inexperience in his business, but because he does not wish to be seen as a taskmaster or slave driver in the real sense of the word, he presents the part of him that apparently confirms his humanity in his state of nobility.

It is like understanding the humanity of a prophet or the Messiah, which is often interpreted as weakness.

This scenario, no doubt, poses a major dilemma for him. How he handles and solves this dilemma informs the outcome of his relationship with the slave. And this is one of the major reasons I am writing this book.

Chapter Three

THE SADDLE

A saddle is a seat placed on the back of a horse or any other animal for the rider. It could also be a seat on a bicycle or motorcycle for the rider. It means a position of control or being in charge. To be in a saddle or sit on a saddle puts one in a place of responsibility. Hence, one can either be given a saddle or he takes it by force. In this chapter, we shall be discussing what the saddle refers to in our contemporary existence, its design, its designer and its designation in a way to suit our message.

<u>What the Saddle Refers</u>

The saddle refers to the seat of leadership. It is a position of authority, influence and responsibility. It refers to an office, a place for exercising leadership ability and tendencies in a proper manner that produces positive impact.

The saddle could also be a throne for a monarch or a bench for a barrister. It could be a pulpit for a pastor, priest or prophet. The saddle could also be a presidential villa for Mr. President or a chamber for the lawmakers. We can refer the saddle to a cockpit for a pilot or a classroom for a teacher.

A security guard at his post or at the gate is on his saddle. A doctor in the hospital, diagnostician in the laboratory, or an architect in the drawing room – all are occupying their saddle. Even the driver of a bus, the rider of a motorbike, and a police man on the road are on their saddle. In a simple term, the saddle is an office.

The Design of the Saddle

It was Myles Munroe who said that purpose determines design, and design determines needs. He also said that it is the manufacturer who determines the design of a product. Since design means both pattern and pilot of a work of art, we will look at how the saddle was made and on what premise it was made.

Having seen what the saddle refers to, we shall look at its design – the premise or basis on which it was made. In order to fully understand the purpose and for whom the saddle was made, there is need to know what was the mind-set of the Designer and the basis for it.

The Saddle Was Designed In Righteousness

Since we refer the saddle to an office, position or throne, we need to understand that God designed it a throne of righteousness. This is to say that every position of influence, every office of administration, and every throne of authority is designed in righteousness and for right doing. This point is very important to underscore our need to treat it with dignity. When an object created or made in righteousness is not seen as such, it loses its dignity and gross abuse becomes imminent and inevitable. So, we must treat any office or position of influence even at the home-front as a sacred post.

Our national and state assemblies are often referred to as Hallowed Chambers. We often hear this in the news. But if you ask an average citizen what they think of that nomenclature in relation to the activities that go on there, the answer you will get may shock you. The truth is that our lawmakers in recent times have not treated their chamber as a hallowed place – both upper and lower chambers. Most often than not, it has been a theatre of supposedly honorable men who are so desperate for power, so self-absorbed and extremely negligent to the plight of the citizenry. We are yet to see righteousness and holiness play out on the floor of the assembly to convince us that it is a hallowed chamber. Godly nomenclature without godly character becomes a label of nonentity and emptiness!

The Saddle Was Designed In Power

Every throne or position of influence and authority which the saddle represents is designed by God in power and strength. Since the Designer is not a weak God, but a God of power, so His design can never be on a weak foundation. Moreover, the saddle being a place of authority cannot be pivoted on weakness. When the structure of any entity is weak, fractures become obvious results. Any saddle that is pitched on a weak frame and foundation cannot exercise authority or dispense justice appropriately and adequately. Hence, the entire system breaks down.

The Bible asked, *"If the foundations are destroyed, what can the [unyieldingly] righteous do, or what has He [the Righteous One] wrought or accomplished?"* (Psalm 11:3 AMP). The New Living Translation, NLT, version puts it thus: *"The foundations of law and order have collapsed. What can the righteous do?"*

This explains why the leadership of our country is weak. It is pitched on a shaky and weak foundation. The saddle can no longer command authority; it can no longer correct impunity, and no longer strong enough to withstand the storms of economic, political and socio-cultural challenges that naturally face any entity.

Most people argue that Nigeria and Africa have not had good men in the corridors of power, but I beg to disagree. Africa has produced men who could turn her fortunes around but they never did. Why is it so? It is because *"The foundations of law and order have collapsed. What can the righteous do?"* Until such foundations are repaired and re-dedicated to the Omni-potent God, even the righteous cannot do much good sitting on the saddle.

A case study is President Saul of ancient Israel. In First Samuel chapter nine and in verse two, it was recorded that Saul was a *"choice young man, and a goodly, and there was not among the children of Israel a goodlier person than he..."*

Look at that! He was a choice young man who was also handsome and taller than all in Israel. Yet, when he mounted the saddle, he failed the Council of Heaven and the sons of men. President Saul was a warrior from the tribe of Benjamin – a tribe famous for their bravery and warrior-spirit, yet Saul became weak in taking a solid stand for God and goodness. The cause? A weak foundation for the saddle!

Since the saddle as originally designed by God is a seat of authority, it is an aberration and abnormality for it to reveal or resonate weakness. Instead, it is expected to reflect power – the power of its Creator. This power is not force because that is what we usually witness. It was when men of error – slaves – mounted the saddle that force was introduced into leadership. Ever since, their successors have continued with the old tradition. Force has been their way. Since they cannot exude the power as originally designed and ordained, they resort to the use of force to execute their mandate. This, unfortunately, is where we find ourselves in this part of the globe.

And this is not good for the great giant of Africa and her sister nations.

The Saddle Was Designed In Meekness

What is meekness? It is the quality of being meek: humble, modest, meagre, or self-effacing. I am not talking about being weak or having low self-esteem. Not at all. But being gentle and generous in the praise of others who are doing well. God inspired Moses to give a true testimony or attestation of himself as *"a quietly humble man, more so than anyone living on Earth"* (Numbers 12:3 TM). Yet, he was not a weak man.

Remember, it was Moses who led a high profile delegation to Pharaoh of Egypt to demand the release of his people, Israel. He also conquered Pharaoh at the Red Sea, conquered all the armies of nations that confronted them in the wilderness. The same Moses was able to quell all internal conflicts in his country especially the notorious rebellion of Korah, Dathan, and Abiram with their 250 member-party in the Book of Numbers chapter sixteen.

So, such a man cannot be described as a weak man. He was simply meek, not because it was in him, (remember he came from the tribe of Levi known for their fierce anger), but because that was the demand of the saddle where God put him.

When we say that every saddle is designed in meekness, we mean that the men who ascend it are naturally and traditionally expected to be shaped by it. The office and its design shape any man who occupies it to consciously and unconsciously conform to it. So, Moses had no choice but to fit in.

Meekness is that quality that reveals true leadership and its origin. Any man who occupies a God-ordained position with the mandate of God and the people will always operate in humility, modesty and quietness. His reign or regime will be marked by great accomplishments because he does not call unnecessary attention to what he is doing. Such a man or woman is not a Pharisee – known for blowing their trumpet. Jesus said, *"Be especially careful when you are trying to be good so that you don't make a performance out of it. It might be a good theatre, but God who made you won't be applauding. When you do something for someone else, don't call attention to yourself. You've seen them in action, I'm sure – 'playactors' I call them..."* (Matthew 6:1-2 TM).

This is a serious caution to those who may be tempted to act too self-important and self-absorbing when they ascend the saddle. On the other hand, He added, *"Here's what I want you to do: Find a quiet, secluded place so you won't be tempted to role-play before God. Just be there as simply and honestly as you can manage. The focus will shift from you to God, and you will begin to sense his grace"* (vs. 6 TM).

What the Master was saying in essence is that grace works in the life of a man or woman who leads, rules, acts or lives in meekness and lowliness of heart. Meekness makes the man on the saddle to *"condescend to men of low estate"* (Romans 12:16). This is because he is of the same mind with those he is leading and does not mind high things. This admonition by Apostle and Teacher Paul is taken seriously by men and women who understand that the saddle on which they sit is designed in meekness.

Jesus Christ did not become arrogant and highhanded in His dealings with human beings because His office or saddle as the Saviour was birthed in meekness. That was why He never used His anointing and grace to demand that His opponents should fall and die. That was why He never employed nor demanded that heaven's police should beat the Pharisees and Sadducees with anointed heaven-made batons or shoot them down with heaven-made AK-47 rifles. This meekness is the key to a successful leadership. This is because that is what the saddle demands based on its design.

Remember the admonition in Romans 12:16 again: *"Live in harmony with one another; do not be haughty (snobbish, high-minded, exclusive), but readily adjust yourself to [people, things] and give yourselves to humble tasks. Never overestimate yourself or be wise in your own conceits"* (AMP). Again, *"with gentleness correcting those who are in opposition, if perhaps God may grant them repentance leading to the knowledge of the truth..."* (2 Timothy 2:25 NASB).

The Saddle Was Designed In the Fear of God

The fear of God is the beginning of wisdom. This statement of truth was made by the wisest president that ever lived. President Solomon David made that submission after realizing that leadership of any great nation like Israel was not, and is still not by muscle or hustle. It is by the wisdom of God. That is why he wrote in Proverbs 24:3-6 thus:

"It takes wisdom to build a house (nation), *and understanding to set it on a firm foundation* (to avoid collapse). *It takes knowledge to furnish its rooms with fine furniture and beautiful draperies. It's better to be wise than strong; intelligence outranks muscle any day. Strategic planning is the key to warfare; to win, you need a lot of good counsel"* (TM.) Emphasis mine

Intelligence, that is, wisdom, knowledge and understanding in a complete pack only comes from the fear of God. The saddle was not designed in the fear of man, but in the fear of God. The fear of man brings torment and breeds troubles and tribulation. The fear of God brings triumph and testimonies of success even in times of trouble. It is very unfortunate that leaders of this present stock swim in the fear of man. The legacy of *godfatherism* is what they are building for future generations.

Men no longer fear the immortal and invisible God, rather, they are filled with the fear of undesirable mortals and are consumed with hero-worship. That is why the political and leadership landscape has been overrun by louts and loud-mouthed desperados who gallivant the towns in the name of political godfathers. Thus, men of supposed intelligence drown in the pool of this ugly political theatrics.

Men who should relish the fear of God now reel to and fro in the fear of men. They relegate the God of all power and delegate men of tiny power and massive error, and most times, elevate them. That is why those who by divine design find themselves on the saddle must tread with caution not to allow the fear of mere mortals truncate their polished destiny.

The reply of President Solomon to God's open check in the Holy Bible Book of First Kings chapter three reveals the heart of a man who has the fear of God. Not only that, he did not ascend the throne or mount the saddle as if it was his right; he did it in reverence to God. It was that fear of God; that consciousness of awe of what God did for him that overwhelmed him to the point that he professed his loyalty to God.

Any man who has no fear of God and mounts the saddle cannot do well in spite of huge investments and enviable resources at his disposal. He will end up a slave! And because he lacks the fear of God, he will constantly live in the fear of men. That was the case with President Saul of Benjamin, Israel.

In First Samuel 15:24, it is written, *"And Saul said unto Samuel, I have sinned: for I have transgressed the commandment of the LORD, and thy words: because I feared the people, and obeyed their voice."* The fear of man is transgression against the LORD! It is a deviation from divine pathways which in turn diminishes both the expectations of God and the people of the country.

One of the reasons God instructed Gideon to send away some people from the army that would confront Midian is fear. *"The Lord said to Gideon, The people who are with you are too many for Me to give the Midianites into their hands...So now proclaim in the ears of the men, saying, Whoever is <u>fearful and trembling</u>, let him turn back and depart from Mount Gilead. And 22,000 of the men returned, but 10,000 remained"* (Judges 7:2-3 AMP).

Look at that! 22,000 fearful soldiers! Fear brings defeat especially when it is the fear of man. Those who must bear rule on the saddle must be strong only by the fear of God. President Saul replaced the fear of God with the fear of the people, and that foolish action cost him the kingship and the kingdom of Israel. Be wise not to do likewise!

The Saddle Was Designed In Integrity

Dictionary defines integrity as "steadfast adherence to a strict moral and ethical code. It is the condition of being complete, pure, wholesome, and unimpaired" in character and conversation. Some of the words to define integrity include honesty, uprightness, rectitude, probity, sincerity, virtue, and decency. When God calls a man to occupy an office of influence, the first requirement is integrity. It is believed that such a man must have the fear of God before the calling.

But one fundamental ingredient needed for God to establish him securely on the throne is his integrity. That was why Genesis 17:1 records,

"When Abram was ninety-nine years old, the Lord appeared to him and said, I am the Almighty God;

walk and live habitually before Me and be perfect (blameless, wholehearted, complete)' AMP.

God further assured him of His covenant with him. He was simply saying: If I, God, must use you to bless the nations of the world, you must be a man of integrity. This is to say that any man who occupies a position of influence but does not have integrity will end up exuding bad influence and will never be a blessing to the people. It is popularly said that he who comes to equity must come with clean hands. The Word of God also asked,

"O Lord, who may abide in Your tent? Who may dwell in Your holy hill? He who walks in integrity, and works righteousness, and speaks truth in his heart" (Psalm 15:1-2 NASB).

If you read through that entire chapter of the Book of Psalms, you will see other ingredients for a life of integrity. These qualify a man to sit on the saddle. So, because the throne is designed in integrity, men and women who ascend it must live the life of integrity.

Integrity preserves the saddle. It lengthens the span of the throne and grants long life to men who sit on it in the integrity of their heart. It attracts honor and glory to the man who sits on it in wholeness of character. But the truth is that integrity does not befit slaves. It is the hallmark of all virtues which only noblemen possess. Integrity is the foundation for quality leadership. Only by it the saddle prospers.

Proverbs 20:28 says, *"Love and truth form a good leader; sound leadership is founded on loving integrity"* (TM).

Looking at that statement of truth closely, you will see the relationship between a good leader (the one who sits on the saddle) and the saddle or stool which provides his leadership. We can see how a good leader, a noble man, is formed or the stuff he is made of. Love of God and love for the people leads him to a life of truthfulness. No one who loves the people lies to them. A loving leader cannot be a lying person. He tells the truth, lives in the truth, and demands the truth from all and sundry. And because he is a man of loving integrity, his saddle is secure.

The Living Bible translation of that statement by President Solomon puts it thus: *"If a king is kind, honest, and fair, his kingdom stands secure."* Most thrones and kingdoms have collapsed because the stool of integrity on which they sat on at the beginning has been destroyed by their lies. The integrity of a man on a throne cannot be overemphasized because the throne as originally established by God was founded on the pillars of truth and integrity. When the pillar of integrity is altered or shifted, collapse becomes inevitable in a matter of time.

The Saddle and Its Designation

We have looked at what the saddle refers to, and its design. Now, we will look at the last point in this chapter – the designation of the saddle. By design here, we have seen what form the saddle is made in and what stuff it is made of. But by designation, we mean and shall be looking at its purpose or what it is made for.

There is a purpose for everything God designed or even the ones that man designed. Nothing in particular exists without a purpose. The Word of God even confirms that even the wicked is made for judgement or condemnation. So, nothing really exists without a reason for its existence. This also applies to the saddle.

Since God is the Designer of the saddle, He is in the best position to tell us the designation of the saddle. To get this information or revelation of what the saddle was meant for, we must consult with the Word of God. Why? *"The Whole Bible was given to us by inspiration of God and is useful to teach us what is true..."* (2 Timothy 3:16a TLB). This is it!

No other record can give us the authentic purpose of the saddle than the Bible. This is because it is the inspiration of God that gave birth to it. It is the Word of God as revealed to the men who put it on record. Any other book could be a commentary of theologians, politicians, psychologists, sociologists, philosophers, etc. Since no man designed the saddle, no man can give a true report of the reason for its design and existence. So, let us take the following from God's report.

The Saddle Is Made For The Purpose Of Extending God's Rule to the Earth

"Then God said, Let us make man in our image, after our likeness; and let them have dominion (or bear rule) over the fish of the sea, and over the birds of the air, and over the cattle, and over all the earth and

over every creeping thing that creeps upon the earth"
(Genesis 1:26 RSV) emphasis mine.

When God created man and put him in a position to exert influence on the earth, He did it for the purpose of extending His divine rule over all things in heaven, on earth and beneath the earth. By this purpose, man became the governor of the earth. However, this privilege to govern the earth was originally to extend God's rule over all creation. Since God is Spirit, it became very necessary to make man in His image and likeness who in flesh and blood would communicate and interact with the physical realm on God's behalf. This was a perfect arrangement by God until sin disrupts that arrangement and system.

"Yet I did spot one ray of light in this murk: God made men and women true and upright; we're the ones who've made a mess of things" (Ecclesiastes 7:29 TM).

Mankind indeed made a mess of things to such an extent that many have been made to believe that the place of leadership is man-made, corrupt and should only be for corrupt men. That is why it is widely believed in this part of the globe that politics is a dirty game only for dirty people. But it is not so from the beginning. God never made any corrupt thing – individuals or institutions – the saddle inclusive. All of God's creation was made pure and perfect, but mankind corrupted them.

The Word of God as recorded in the Holy Bible affirms that God is the Governor amongst the nations. Psalm 22:28 *"For the kingdom is the LORD's: and he is the governor among the nations"*. Psalm 99:1 says, *"The Lord reigns. Let the peoples tremble..."* (NASB).

I love The Message Bible rendering of that portion: *"God rules. On your toes, everybody! He rules from his angel throne – take notice! God looms majestic in Zion, He towers in splendour over all the big names..."*

God rules over all the big names you can think of in all the nations of the world. This means that whatever office or position anyone may occupy, they are under God. Apostle Paul wrote to the Roman Christians to *"be a good citizen. All governments are under God. Insofar as there is peace and order, it's God's order."* (Romans 13:1 TM).

This is to say that God puts people in the saddle of leadership or positions of influence as His regents. And when they fail, he holds them accountable. Read this: *"I commissioned you judges, each one of you, deputies of the high God. But you've betrayed your commission..."* (Psalm 82:6-7 TM). So, you can see that the saddle is for the extension of divine government and rule.

The Saddle Was Made To Create Law And Order.

First Corinthians chapter fifteen verse thirty three says, *"For God is not a God of confusion but of peace"* (RSV). This means that God is not the author of disorder. He is not glorified in an atmosphere of disorder. There is disorder when there is a breakdown of law and order. Any house divided against itself cannot stand. United we stand, divided we fall.

For there to be order in any organization, community or country, laws are made by those who occupy the saddle. The laws are not made by the followers, they are made by the leaders who are elected or appointed or selected to represent the people in certain capacities. When these leaders make the laws, all and sundry are required by the provisions of the law to observe and keep them – the leaders inclusive. But a situation where those who occupy privileged positions fail to make good laws that would ensure peace and order in the land, there is neglect. Or where they fail to observe and keep the laws themselves, they abuse their office and anarchy looms in the land.

When God created the first humans, He designed an office for them. Then, it was Adam, the Man. God assigned him a position of influence as an extension of His rule on earth. Adam had his job descriptions: To cultivate the Garden of Eden (NASB), *"to work the ground and to keep it in order"* (TM.) – Genesis 2:15. So, what his office was designed for was to work the ground or the garden and ensure order was maintained in that environment. This means that he was to do his work as a farmer and protect the environment under his jurisdiction as the chief security officer.

So, whether as a parent at the home front, a manager in the office, a director in an agency, an honorable representative in the local government, state or national assembly, a governor or president – your office is designated for law and order. More so in a democratic setting where the rule of law is expected to flourish, those in authority should do all in their constitutional power to keep law and order in the state. But unfortunately, slaves do not believe in the rule of law because they know it does not favor them nor support their selfish cravings.

To buttress the fact that God makes leaders or puts people in positions of influence and leadership for law and order to reign and prevail in their domain, the Queen of Sheba said this to President Solomon of Israel:

"It's all true! Your reputation for accomplishment and wisdom that reached all the way to my country is confirmed. And blessed be God, your God, who took such a liking to you and made you king. Clearly, God's love for Israel is behind this, making you king to keep <u>a just order</u> and <u>nurture a God-pleasing people</u>" (1 Kings 10:6-9 TM emphasis mine).

The noble woman explicitly stated why God makes leaders; why He created the office of influence and impact through quality leadership. One of the reasons she pointed out to His Excellency, President Solomon was **"to keep a just order".** A just order means a good and fair government. It does not really indicate a society void of irregularities, but a leadership that is upright and void of injustice and corruption. It is such a leadership that quite contrasts what is obtained in most of our present day African countries.

Where there is law and order, corruption is alien. Impunity becomes a stranger that is not welcomed by the people. But a government void of law and order becomes a breeding ground and safe haven for all manners of vices and atrocities.

One of my favorite political analysts and social commentators on radio, Barrister Jide Ologun always says, **"If you make room for lawlessness, the law will be crippled."** Our leaders must be careful not to allow themselves be completely taken over by the spirit of this error whereby law and order flee from their lands, which is almost becoming the prevailing scenario in our countries in Africa.

The Saddle Was Made To Execute Justice

"Praise the Lord your God who delights in you and has placed you on the throne (saddle) of Israel (Nigeria). Because of the Lord's eternal love for Israel (Nigeria), he has made you king (president, governor, legislator, chairman, director, traditional leader, parent, etc.) so you can rule with justice and righteousness" (1 Kings 10:9 NLT, emphasis mine).

Every enlightened and educated person knows that one of the functions of leadership is to dispense justice and execute judgement appropriately. The good man is rewarded with praise while the wicked man is rewarded with punishment. The righteous and patriotic citizen is applauded and showered with honors while the compromising and unfaithful citizen is penalized according to the law.

When Lucifer, the head of the first angelic estate failed Heaven which was his constituency and God his Leader, God did not pamper him or grant him amnesty. He punished him according to His righteousness. God gave the order and His Angels pushed the unpatriotic Lucifer down from his high office. (See Revelations 12:7-9). God did not do that to show off to the heavenly realm and the world that He is God. Not at all! He did that to keep a just, righteous and organized estate. Everyone in leadership position ought to learn from God and do the same. Men created in God's image and likeness should emulate Him.

Jesus Christ told the people of His day this: ***"The Son can do nothing by himself. He does only what he sees the Father doing, and in the same way"*** (John 5:19 TLB). So, since God the Father designed the saddle where you sit on, you should follow His example in doing things. He is the God of justice, you too should be a man of justice. This is a very crucial essence of every leader's election.

When leaders do not dispense justice in the right way, they eventually corrupt it. When they do not penalize the erring people or punish criminals according to the sovereign law of God and of the state, the land becomes a breeding ground for crime and corruption, hence more criminals arise. Their inability to allow the heavy and long arm of the law to deal with criminals emboldens and empowers those criminals to freely run the town. This is another serious bane of our nation, which has earned us disruptive and distressing moments across the land.

When innocent people do not get justice in the law courts and fair treatment in public squares, the land becomes a haven for impunity to thrive. People would begin to take laws into their hands. The poor and defenseless would begin to devise frantic means to defend themselves. That is why our country's justice system is in shambles. The gavel in both the houses of assembly and the court of law has become a tool for self-service.

Justice is denied the innocent and sold out to the guilty who can pay for it. This is an aberration of the character of the saddle. All these happen because the corridors of power, authority and influence are nowadays occupied by slaves who have no understanding of its purpose as originally ordained by God.

The slow and sluggish manner legal matters are being handled in our country leaves much to be desired of those saddled with the responsibility of providing justice. The judges are slow because they have been paid to drag their feet in giving verdict, and when they finally give it, they favor the rich and dismiss the case filed by the poor "for lack of merit" – merit only defined by them.

In all these, my joy is that heaven is not keeping quiet over these abnormalities and irregularities. The Psalmist wrote: "God calls the judges into his courtroom, he puts all the judges in the dock. *'Enough! You've corrupted justice long enough, you've let the wicked get away with murder. <u>You're here to defend the defenseless, to make sure that underdogs get a fair break; your job is to stand up for the powerless, and prosecute all those who exploit them"</u>* (Psalm 82:1-4 TM, emphasis mine).

Take a second look at the underlined in that scriptural quote above, which is what the saddle is meant to project. This does not apply only to the justice system or the judiciary, but to all those who by privilege find themselves in one position or the other in every sector or industry. When justice is rightly served, it shows that the right people are in charge. The absence of this vital essence of leadership is an indication that the wrong people are running the system – slaves, probably.

The Saddle Was Designed For Righteousness

Righteousness has two main definitions. One is holiness which is the divine nature of God. Another is the act of living or being right. Here, we shall be discussing righteousness in the light of works. That is, the works of righteousness. Everyone created in God's image is required by divine law to do righteousness. This is the act or conduct of one who is righteous in God's eyes. We are created for good works.

In Acts of the Apostles chapter ten and verses thirty-four and thirty-five, Peter said, *"Of a truth I perceive that God is no respecter of persons: but in every nation he that feareth him, and worketh righteousness, is accepted with him."* Apostle Peter said this while reporting on the conversion of an army officer, a captain in the army of Rome who feared God. He was simply telling the other apostles and Christian believers back at Jerusalem that *"those who worship God and do good deeds are acceptable to God"* (TLB), irrespective of their nationality. Good deeds should, thus, proceed from the throne.

God designed the place of authority for men to do good deeds. A leader is a servant, in fact, the chief servant in his domain or environment of influence. His office places a demand on him to initiate, develop, and execute programs and projects that will translate in alleviating pain and poverty in the lives of those he leads. Apostle Paul wrote, *"The authorities are God's servants for your good..."* (Romans 13:4a NLT). This means that those who are in authority are required by design and designation of their office to do good works. Failure to do this is an abuse of office.

Leaders are agents of good works. Only a few good men, though, realize that the reason they ascend the throne, are elected into office or appointed to lead is for the people and not for themselves. The Holy Bible history records this:

"So, David became greater and greater, for the Lord God of heaven was with him. Then King Hiram of Tyre sent cedar lumber, carpenters and masons to build a palace for David. David now realized why the Lord had made him the king and blessed his kingdom so greatly – it was because God wanted to

pour out his kindness on Israel, his chosen people" (2 Samuel 5:10-12 TLB).

Can we say this of any of our presidents, governors, senators and representatives in the houses of assembly? Would posterity find somewhere in the future where it would be written about our chairmen, directors, federal ministers and state commissioners that they realized why God placed them in leadership positions? Even now, is there anywhere we could find where it is written of the past leaders that they came to a point of realization that God gave them the seat of authority because He wanted to use them and pour out His kindness on Nigerians and Africans?

Or are you not wondering why there are no such records about the past leaders existing anywhere in our contemporary history? Only a few have been reported as men who tried to do good. A handful of others tried to follow in that noble path but were never allowed to execute their noble plans. However, the percentage difference of the few good men and the unpatriotic majority is as wide as the gulf between heaven and hell. And this is worrisome!

No office exists for formality sake. No throne exists as a mere monument or museum. No position of influence is designed or designated for the decoration of those who occupy them. All these exist for productive performance, not panorama! The anointing is not for announcement, but for accomplishment. The title is not for tithe or tax, but for tasks. Every unction is given for function and not for fun.

President David realized that it was because of what God designed to fulfil in the lives of his people that he was made commander in chief. The task to be accomplished is the reason for the throne and the title! If all men knew this, there would be no selfish leaders on the throne, only serving leaders! Bible history has this record about a one-time president and commander in chief of Israel:

"Then Hezekiah the king went to work: He got all the leaders of the city together..." (2 Chronicles 29:20 TM).

This is what leaders are expected to do – to work! This is what noblemen are put in charge to do – to work! This can only happen when they are in charge.

Noblemen work and strengthen themselves with food in order to do more work. Slaves party and get drunk while the work suffers. This is because they are hired servants, and hired servants are usually lazy and indolent. They hate to work for others.

Jesus Christ said something very crucial and worth meditating on: *"A hired man is not a real shepherd. The sheep mean nothing to him. He sees a wolf and runs for it, leaving the sheep to be ravaged and scattered by the wolf. He's only in it for the money. The sheep don't matter to him"* (John 10:12-13 TM).

So if you are one of those privileged to be leaders in any given capacity and environment, remember, your first job is to initiate, plan and execute projects that will touch the lives of the people in meeting their needs and to establish a prosperous economy.

The Saddle Was Designated For Providing Economic Boom and Prosperity

The first blessing God pronounced upon man after creation was the blessing of prosperity (Genesis 1:28 TM). God decreed fruitfulness on the man. Fruitfulness is a command, not a suggestion. *"God blessed them: 'Prosper! Reproduce! Fill earth! Take charge!'..."* (Verse 28 TM). According to this passage of Bible history, God Almighty the Designer of the saddle gave man a charge to prosper, produce and fill the earth.

Now, the question is, what should man prosper in? What is he to produce? And with what is he to fill the earth? The Amplified Version of the Holy Bible of the same text explains: *"...Be fruitful, multiply, and fill the earth and subdue it [using all its vast resources in the service of God and man]..."* Look at that last line again: **"using all its vast resources in the service of God and man"**. That is what the command summarizes.

The mandate on any leader at any level puts him in a position to provide certain services and amenities to his people. Whatever the services may be – spiritual, economic, social, cultural, diplomatic, scientific, etc. – they should translate to the prosperity of the people and the land. This is what the office or position of influence demands; that one who is in charge uses all the vast resources available in the community or country to bring about prosperity in the land and to the people. But unfortunately, this has not been so in this country and the continent.

The best we have witnessed is the growth in the GDP and economy without enhancing the living standard of the people. Our economies only grow on the pages of fiscal reports but reflect the opposite in our lives. What is responsible for this is that the people in charge do not know how to translate the recorded growth from the pages of financial reports to positively affect the lives of the people.

One crucial point that is worthy of note is that prosperity is a function of investment. Not just investment, but quality investment. It is quality investment that yields quality harvest. Without investment, there is no harvest. We can only harvest when we invest! And more importantly, what we invest determines what we harvest. There is no miracle rod or magic wand that can produce prosperity without investment.

These investments must be properly channeled and directed towards productivity. The land and her people cannot prosper if the investment is taken outside their territory. Nigeria and Africa are poor not because they have no vast resources or good business men and investors, but because most of the investments are taken outside and vast resources that should make them world-class are neglected.

When investments are taken outside the country, jobs are created for foreigners while the citizens become idle. The net result is that they engage in worthless pursuits and even in crime. What we have witnessed so far is mass looting of the nation's treasury by those in authority. More worrisome is the fact that they take these loots to other countries and invest them there.

Presidents, governors, senators, directors, chairmen of commissions, directors of government agencies, federal ministers, state commissioners and many others in privileged positions of leadership have continued to betray their commissions by embezzling our collective patrimony and leaving the country and her people impoverished and hungry. All these are happening because the leaders do not understand the designation of the saddle they sit on. Even those of them who understand this part of their responsibility become either demonically distracted, devilishly selfish or deviously defiant to the needs of the people. Too bad that it makes me sad!

In providing economic boom and prosperity which every position of influence or leadership is ordained for, the leaders who count themselves noblemen should constantly seek ways to productively and creatively invest the vast resources God at creation generously provided for us. Any administration that must meet the human need for economic freedom is required to do the needful – provide the atmosphere and platform for both local and foreign investors to develop the fundamental infrastructures necessary for growth and prosperity.

The government must draft policies and design programs and projects to generate this compulsory economic boom. When this happens, the peaceful coexistence of citizens across the country becomes less sermonized. We spend much unnecessary time, energy and other valuably scarce resources to harp on peaceful coexistence and the need for all to tolerate one another because those saddled with this basic responsibility of providing platforms for peace, prosperity and progress are careless, callous and arrogantly pursuing their own selfish agenda. This brazenly wicked attitude is befitting of a slave – an error that must be corrected if things must go well with us.

The Saddle Was Designated For Providing Security of Lives and Property

One of the assignments God gave Adam in the Garden of Eden was to provide security around it. *"And the Lord God took the man and put him in the Garden of Eden to tend and guard and keep it"* (Genesis 2:15 AMP). God is the Chief Security Officer of the Universe while Man is that of the earth. But it is not enough to bear the nomenclature; the duty should be understood and undertaken. The task is more important than the title!

Here in our land, we have people who sit as chief of army, chief of defense, of navy, of air-force, and even as chief of police, yet the crime rate is grossly alarming. Governors receive security votes yet kidnapping and ritual killings go on notoriously unchecked in their states. In most cases, the security personnel are even involved in these notoriously nefarious and demeaning activities. What a shame that common cases of social miscreants threatening the sovereign unity of the country go unsolved and unchecked with heavy sums of tax-payers money invested annually in security.

When people saddled with the responsibility of providing security fail, the economy suffers. Prospective and potential investors stay off any territory that is infested with crime as a result of breakdown in security. And when investment cannot be attracted, economy falls into a comatose, the prospects of prosperity becomes elusive and unattainable. Prosperity can only be achieved in an atmosphere of peace and environment of safety. This is why those whose duty it is to secure lives and property in the nation should do so in consideration that it is their divine assignment, and an important designation of their office.

Most times, security of lives and property fails because security agencies lack these two basics according to Nehemiah 7:1-2. *"After the wall was finished and I had set up the doors in the gates, the gatekeepers, singers, and levites were appointed. I gave the responsibility of governing Jerusalem to my brother Hanani along with Hananiah, the commander of the fortress, for he was a faithful man who feared God more than most."* Faithfulness and the fear of God are key attributes of good security officers. Nehemiah knew this fact, and when he saw these qualities in Hanani his brother and in Hananiah the ruler of the city, he quickly put them in charge.

When a security officer lacks the fear of God, he can allow a breach in security which in turn jeopardizes the chances of a city or country flourishing in peace and prosperity. The lack of the fear of God and honesty has put our dear country and her economy in many a dicey situations. Goods meant for the citizens are smuggled out to neighboring countries.

Daily and weekly newspaper reports reveal the decay in our security system. Cases of diversions of crude oil or refined products from our country to other African states attest to the porous nature of our security. Human and drug trafficking also speak negatively of this wickedness that proceed from those in charge of our security. And until these men and women realize that where they sit is meant to protect lives and property and thereby facilitate prosperity, these ugly trends will continue to evade our lives and hinder our progress.

Chapter Four

THE SWITCH

'There is another evil I have seen under the sun. Kings and rulers make a grave mistake when they give great authority to foolish people and low position to people of proven worth'– Ecclesiastes 10 verses 5 & 6 New Living Translation).

We have successfully explained who slaves and their drivers are in the context of this book. We have equally seen their characteristics as well as what they do. So far, we have looked at the saddle – what it represents, its design and designation. Now, we shall look at the crux of the matter that led me into writing this book.

You may consider all that had been said so far as preamble to the central point we are about to delve into. I am sure you would not quickly agree with me that they are just preamble. Well, just making my mind known to you. God helping me, I will be as mild as I can in putting forth the truth and fundamental facts here for our enlightenment and learning.

The writer of the Book of Ecclesiastes who was the wisest man that ever lived, (of course, apart from our Lord and Saviour Jesus Christ who is Wisdom personified) wrote several centuries before Christ the words in chapter ten verses five and six: *"There is another evil I have seen under the sun"*, he said. *"Kings and rulers make a grave mistake when they give great authority to foolish people* (slaves) *and low positions to people of proven worth* (nobles)." Emphasis mine. This evil he saw is what I call the Switch.

A switch is a change in position. It is a diversion or digression from the norm. It could be a positive or negative switch. A positive switch is when darkness is turned into light, for instance, or when poverty turns into prosperity. Positive switch is when recession turns to procession or progression or boom. When these happen, there is joy and jubilation in the city or country as when a wicked leader is removed and a righteous man takes his place. This is usually described as good development.

But a negative switch is the opposite of all that I have highlighted above about a positive switch. A negative switch is what President Solomon David referred to as "evil" in his treatise, Ecclesiastes or The Preacher. And this is one evil I see in Africa, which we need to find a way to fix urgently and without further delay. I will always make strong reference to Nigeria, the acclaimed giant of Africa.

According to our text which forms the buttress for my argument in this chapter, this switch is allowed by **"king and rulers"**. Now, who are the kings and rulers? In Solomon's time, they were the ruling class; people like himself. This is because it was a time when monarchs ruled the state. But in the context of this book and in a democratic setting, kings and rulers are actually the noblemen as I described in previous chapter.

According to Abraham Lincoln, democracy is the government of the people, by the people, and for the people. And this is somewhat a direct democracy. This means that they can choose who represents them, speaks for them and act on their behalf as in a representative democracy, which is what Nigeria and most African countries practice.

So, if we take Abraham Lincoln's definition wholly, it agrees that the people who are the government are the kings and rulers in our context. This also implies that whoever they choose to speak or act on their behalf in matters of diplomacy or legislature become their servants. These servants either choose to be hired hands or slaves. This classification or categorization depends on how they, that is, the servants in general choose to relate with their true masters – the people. But this is not our headache. The trouble is the switch which we have seen that was allowed by the "kings and rulers", the people who are the true government. Why is this so?

Kings and rulers are saddled with the responsibility or duty of providing guidance and direction for things to run smoothly in any given society. They are endowed to create an atmosphere and conducive environment for progress and unity in the state.

The Trigger of the Switch

Now, how did these kings and rulers lose their grip on the saddle that led to the switch? Were they apparently overthrown or was the saddle hijacked by trick? Did they willingly but ignorantly surrender their original position to these servants-turned-lords? Were they hypnotized by rhetoric or flattery? Or was it a careless but foolish mistake? In any case, this grave mistake is responsible for where we are in the Cush continent; in the ugly situation where slaves rule and masters ruin.

From President Solomon's preaching in the Book of Ecclesiastes chapter ten, he identified some sensitive, but often ignored or overlooked obvious reasons for this switch. Remember, he pointed out that this switch or error or grave mistake proceeds from those in charge – the kings and rulers. He said,

"Dead flies cause the ointment of the perfumer to putrefy [and] send forth a vile odor. So does a little folly [in him who is valued for wisdom] out-weighs wisdom and honor" (vs. 1 AMP).

This submission indicates that a little foolishness or the display of foolishness even in minute degree can mess the wisdom of the wise and honorable men. Kings and rulers are vaunted for their wisdom, yet "a little folly" can vaporize that wisdom no matter how deep the wisdom is.

For better understanding, let me bullet these factors that lead to this evil or switch as follows:

FOOLISHNESS

This is a situation where people who are expected to show wisdom begin to display the opposite. It is also disappointing to see this in people who are valued for wisdom according to President Solomon. Two basic conditions lead to foolishness in people, which eventually subject them to the ruling by others.

One is **ignorance** and the other is **immaturity**. Most Africans on whose shoulders rests the government according to the dictates of democracy are simply naïve and ignorant. And this ignorance has subjected them to undue slavery and hardship in their God-blessed motherland. This unfortunate development can be easily identified in our youths – young people born from the close of the 20th century to the present 21st century. They have no sound knowledge of history and are not eager to study it.

Some of them that I have encountered in the course of my work and interactions with young people are too proud to submit to tutelage and training while a few others do not seem interested in the past. Some of them claim to know so much but show so little of what they claim to know. That is why they become easy targets of cultism, *rascalism*, vulgarism and vagabondism.

The older generation of their fathers and grandfathers and their contemporaries who have been on the saddle decade after decade find them vulnerable tools for manipulating the system. These people who are expected to drive the economy, decide the flow of the wind of politics and change the trajectory of our collective existence become nothing but machines in the hands of the more knowledgeable olden elite class. This is rather very unfortunate and makes me sad, to say the least.

When I look at today's youths, I sigh. When I discuss with them, and see the shallowness of their intellect, intelligence and sense of history, I weep for my country. Only a fraction of them makes sense. Yet, this fraction seems to be engulfed and overwhelmed by the chaotic atmosphere prevailing in the land. But then, engage them and try to help them, Oh, they try to prove that they do not need a lecture on what to do. Little wonder the older generation finds it a mission impossible to trust them with leading the nation. And this has contributed to the unnecessary evil of recycling the old hands in leadership.

The difference between the 21st century youths and those of our time is that we were always eager to learn from our elders. We were always hungry for more. We did not have a social media or internet, but every piece of paper – newspaper, magazine, newsletter, and so on – that came our way, we cherished, devoured, assimilated into our minds, and used in conversations and articles.

But today, our youths have the internet – news at their beck and call; at their door steps every minute of the day, yet many of them are full of ignorance. They receive free data from internet and mobile phone service providers, yet they lavish most of it chatting away, fighting and cursing one another on social media. What an absurd way to treat the generosity of technology! So, how could they see the evil that President Solomon saw going on under the sun? And if they do not see it, how can they start thinking of correcting the debacle?

Not quite long ago, former Nigeria's President Olusegun Obasanjo called on the youths to wrest power from their old people. Many people had criticized him for not doing this while he was in office from 1999 to 2007. But I do not have problem with the time of this solemn call. My problem is that the youths he had called upon to take over the reins of authority in the country do not even understand that they have the power to do so. For void of confusion, according to United Nations, a youth is one between the ages of 18 to 40 years.

Now, looking at our population, this age bracket account for more than the older people. Yet, they are only a handful in government. It is such a pity that the youngest minister in the cabinet of our President Muhammad Buhari is far above 40 years. Even the Minister of Youths and Sports who we had expected to be within the youth age bracket was about 48 years at the time of appointment in September 2015.

I can inform you for free that his appointment was not based on what he could deliver to the youths of the country, but on the premise as one of the loyalists to the ruling political party. Then what happens to the youths of the country he was appointed to represent and serve? A country where the Ambassador to the United States of America is about 80 years old! What a switch! This is all a result of ignorance and laxity on the part of those valued for wisdom.

The other obvious factor that depicts foolishness is immaturity. Apostle Paul writes:

"But remember this, that if a father dies and leaves great wealth for his little son, that child is not much better off than a slave until he grows up, even though he actually owns everything his father had. He has to do what his guardians and managers tell him to until he reaches whatever age his father set" (Galatians 4:1-2 TLB).

This is one cardinal reason slaves are ruling the real and true owners of the land! Immaturity! And until they grow up, become mature, they will continue to be under "tutors and governors" who are described as slaves.

Now, look at what is written about the little son and his managers. Paul said that as long as he is immature, he is no different from a slave. So he has to be under guardians or people who drive him, tell him what to do and where to go. Instead of he who owns the inheritance to dictate what goes on in the estate, the people who should take orders from him dictate for him. This is the switch I am talking about. An evil that is almost a perpetual trend in this part of the globe!

Why is this so painful to my heart? President Solomon the wisest said, *"It doesn't seem right for a fool to succeed or for a slave to rule over princes!"* (Proverbs 19:10 TLB). If this is so, why then are slaves ruling over princes? Paul said, *"Let me show you… As long as the heir is a minor, he has no advantage over the slave"* (Galatians 4:1 TM).

As long as Nigerian masses remain babes, displaying immaturity and exuding ignorance, they will continue to be under guardians and governors who treat them like slaves! That is why Nigerian masses must grow up! And fast too!

The immaturity that is evidently seen in our Nigerian and African youths and even in adults has been the feeder of guts to the politicians in our fatherland. Instead of confronting issues and engaging these over-pampered politicians in constructive debates over how the nation should be governed, these naïve masses fight one another foul on social media and on the streets. It is this regrettable development that is responsible for the high level of ignorance of these masses in core national issues that affect all of us.

Immaturity makes it difficult for people to see what is wrong with a system or structure. Even when they identify the problem, they are prevented by their poor knowledge from knowing the right steps to take to address the problem. No wonder President Solomon observed: *"Fools on the road have no sense of direction. The way they walk tells the story: 'There goes the fool again!"*

It is not just by their fruit or work that you know them, but by their steps too. It is written all over them. So these greedy, self-serving politicians see it and take advantage of it. This is because *"a servant (slave) who acts wisely will rule over a son who acts shamefully, and will share in the inheritance among brothers"* (Proverbs 17:2 NASB). And that will lead me to another factor that breeds a switch.

BODY LANGUAGE

This term has been widely used in the current government of Nigeria led by President Muhammadu Buhari. In fact, before he was elected as President and Commander in Chief of the Armed Forces of the Federal Republic of Nigeria, journalists and political analysts used the term "Body Language" to describe the many moves of the man. It was severally analyzed that the body language of Mr. President revealed he would fight corruption and ensure the supremacy of the rule of law in the country. How true that has been should be for Nigerians to judge. I just wanted to use that to buttress my point in this piece.

Though if you ask me of my opinion about the anti-corruption campaign of Mr. President, I would tell you for free and from a very free mind that it has been, at best, more a fight to recover looted funds than to "kill corruption". This is because some of the people who corrupted Nigeria were nominated and approved to serve in the cabinet of Mr. President. That is by the way.

Now, back to the issue of body language. From my earlier reference to Mr. President's much-publicized body language, we can see that body language is a factor that decides actions or reactions and that provokes comments and analysis, and the overall perception of other people.

The Preacher, President Solomon, said it well: ***"Fools on the road have no sense of direction. The way they walk tells the story..."***

Now, back to the question: Why are slaves ruling over the masters? Why are servants lords over sons? The reason amongst many is that the sons sold out themselves through their body language. If you see a man who is hungry and desperate for food not minding how he gets it, he is an easy prey or target for slaves or servants who are also desperate to hijack his throne. So both of them become slave-minded. Esau, the son of Isaac and elder brother of Jacob is a good example of a slave-minded free-born son.

The throne was his by reason of his position of birth as the firstborn. He was also a hard working young man with a bright future and great prospects. But his body language betrayed him and sold him out as a slave. He was so hungry that his body language revealed his desperation for food. So, upon his request for Jacob's stew, he ignorantly sold out his birth-right to rule as the firstborn of the family and future nation.

As a matter of fact, it was not Esau's utterance or what he said that gave Jacob the nerves to ask for the sale of his birth-right, it was his body language. Esau's body language signaled his readiness to do just anything to get Jacob's stew. His later confession that he was starving to death was only a verbal endorsement of his foolishness. Remember what President Solomon said, *"...The way he walks tells the story"*. Not his words this time, but his walk.

You may have heard people say it severally: Walk your talk. That is, do what you say; practice what you preach. But before things are said, they have been concluded in the mind. So, speaking out is an endorsement of the conclusion of the heart. No wonder Jesus Christ said, *"Out of the abundance of the heart, the mouth speaks."*

I read a story about a young man in the USA who went to a tattoo shop to have certain words tattooed on his body. The tattoo man asked him why he wanted such negative words that revealed low self-esteem carved on his skin. A friend of the shop owner quickly cut in: "Before he left home, he has already carved that on his mind. Whether you put those words there or not makes no difference; he has already concluded that about himself" (paraphrased). How true!

Truth is, the body language of an average Nigerian or African on the street speaks of apathy, self-pity and hopelessness. If you look closely, you will see defeat and despair written all over the faces of the typical Nigerian citizen. Try to engage them in conversation on a national issue especially with regards to politics, economy, or any other key sector that is always in the news, their response would shock you. You would begin to wonder how these folks would survive the current unfriendly realities with such mind-set. I mean, if no drastic attempt is made to put things in the right perspective, they may continue like this forever.

That is why anywhere I find people who are willing to listen – bus terminals, parks, church, markets, etc., – I try to engage them in constructive reasoning. Most times, it is difficult to get them to see from the right perspective because they have been conditioned to see things from where they are such that they do not wish to shift ground to see from other angles.

This is what happens when people are tortured for a long time; when those in charge do not pay attention to the state of their followers. I weep in my heart each time I remember this. Even some of the people who claim that they went to school or have some education, you could imagine the degree of their ignorance which questions the authenticity of the academic degrees they have obtained from the school.

Come to think of it: Why would our leaders in this country continue to hold sway in the face of their evident incompetence in leadership and resource management? Why would political office holders be so bold to hold us in brazen contempt even at the backdrop of their dismal failure to keep their campaign promises? The singular answer is that they watch us, observe us, and listen to what we would say, and then make their decisions as well as take their actions. Our body language as citizens tell them the story: We are not serious!

Though we talk tough at one time, at another time we collapse under the light weight of their deception. When they read us, they see that we are not as serious as our threats, our complaints or our ranting. It is all in our body language. So they take the power from us. They use it against us. They push us to pitch against one another. They enslave us. We moan. We groan. We murmur. We grumble. They smile and shine; smiling to the banks with our collective patrimony which they loot with impunity. We go on social media and make some noise. They reply us by creating distraction and diversions, and we fall cheap by talking back and forth at one another.

And when I see this happen, I remember the observation of the wisest president and commander in chief of God-chosen nation: *"... The way they walk tells the story: 'There goes the fool again!'"* This is one of the reasons we have the switch where slaves now sit on the throne in this part of the globe. An error that the original owners of the land – the kings – allowed to be.

PANIC

It is said in our local parlance that *"Pikin we him papa send go thief, dey use confidence break door"*. This means that a son or child sent by his father to steal, breaks the door with confidence and boldness. The elders who invented this adage did not do so to encourage stealing but to teach that a child can dare even the most unthinkable missions with a strong backing of his father or an elder. Now, let us put it in a saner perspective. If you do not know that your actions are backed up by the law, you panic at the slightest threat or cheap blackmail. The ignorant, average African falls prey to this.

One of the propaganda tools competitors in business or politics use is to incite panic among the consumers of their products or followers respectively. For the business community, the theory is to create fear amongst their customers and consumers of their products to either rush to patronize them more or withdraw patronage from their competitors. For the politicians, they use it to prompt the populace to take action that would work in their favor or react in such a way that would drag the people further into slavery under their rule. The wisest president again cautioned: *"If a ruler loses his temper against you, don't panic: a calm disposition quiets intemperate rage"* (Ecclesiastes 10:4 TM).

When a ruler (not a leader) loses his temper, he has two basic things in mind. One is to put fear in you that the worst has or is about to happen. Two is to push you into the valley of vulnerability. That is, a condition of being weak or poorly defended so you could acknowledge his leadership over you. This is one wicked weapon our leaders even law enforcement agents have repeatedly used to enslave us. They bark as if they are going to bite, roar as if they will devour us, and lash out at us as if without them, we are nothing.

And when this happens, you see an uninformed youth or elder develop cold feet and feeble knees. They begin to shake and stammer like a mouse in a cat convention, trying to explain why they transgressed his lord's commandment. But President Solomon strongly advised, *"... don't panic!"* But will they listen to that advice?

Something happened to me in February 1997 at an area of Lagos, the largest commercial city in Africa.

It was on a Sunday morning and I was on board a commuter bus going to church. I was about 22 years old then but naturally looked younger than my age that one would think I was 18. Just after a short distance down the road, four uniformed police men armed with AK-47 rifles stopped our bus and demanded for some money. But the driver tried to explain to them why he would not be able to part with the money, which they called "roger" – a compulsory illegal toll fee usually extorted by armed men on the roads.

Enraged by that early Sunday morning sermon which they were not ready to listen to, they ordered the bus man to pull over and park his bus. Now, this is usually the part I do not like to see in such unscripted drama. So, while all other passengers looked on and said nothing, I interrupted their unnecessary interrogation of the driver by letting out my utter displeasure. As expected, it attracted the attention of those misinformed uniformed policemen. They shifted their attention from the adamant driver to me – a young boy in their calculation, though wearing a fairly expensive, well-tailored light green-colored three-piece American suit and carrying a brown-leather King James Version of the Holy Bible.

All the commuters were then forced to alight as they threatened to take the driver and his bus to a police station. But my voice grew louder as I engaged those four men in a debate over our constitutional right which they were abusing with impunity. They threatened to pick me up, take me to their Special Anti-Robbery Squad station in the state and lock me up there. They even boasted that they had my types who were languishing in pain and peril in that detention facility. Yet, I did not blink nor bulge as I challenged them in the name of God to dare. Finally, they let us go.

Though the driver was obviously in a state of fear watching the free-to-air movie, owing to the usual experiences of bus drivers in the hands of irate force men. Yet he was grateful that someone was bold enough to stand up to those ill-behaved public officers. That was just one of the many episodes of my ordeals in the hands of unpatriotic public servants. Again, Solomon wisely but strongly advised, *"...don't panic!"*, for they are not more than they really are.

Now, someone may ask: What if I show resistance like you Chris, and find myself in a worse situation? Correction, please: I did not show resistance; I only stood up for my right in a godly and civil manner. They did not come to arrest me else I would have first asked for their warrant and if shown to me, I would follow them to their station. They were public servants – our servants, who should be protecting our rights to free movement, but instead were violating it. They already knew they were wrong but you know, would never admit before you. So they would put up some threats to cow you and make you panic. But for someone like me that already knew their "little secret", they were careful not to provoke the unknown. So, you do not need to resist them, but if you choose to, do it civilly and godly.

But then, hear this: ***"Do your best, prepare for the worst – then trust God to bring victory"*** (Proverbs 21:31 TM).

Secondly, Prophet Jeremiah admonished in Lamentations 3:30: ***"Don't run from trouble. Take it full-face. The "worst" is never the worst"*** (TM.)

Yet you ask, What if the trouble is such that I may not come out alive? Listen again:

"Why? Because the master won't ever walk out and fail to return... He takes no pleasure in making life hard, in throwing roadblocks in the way: stomping down hard on luckless prisoners, refusing justice to victims in the court of High God, tampering with evidence..." (Lamentations 3:31-36 TM).

Did you read that through? God is with you as long you are innocent, and He will fight for you no matter how tough the situation might be. That is why you should make Him your strongest ally and partner and no man dares exert upon you needlessly. Remember what I quoted at the beginning. A child sent by his father to rob breaks the door with confidence. Let alone one who is backed by God Almighty the Father and the sovereign law of the land.

Now, you agree that God is ever faithful but still argue that the "sovereign law" is weak and asks: Who follows due process of the law these days? Do not worry; do your best and God handles the rest, but stand your ground on what is right and fair.

Why? It is because, according to the wisest president, the anger of these slaves is an intemperate one.

The word 'intemperate' means 'lacking moderation, temper or control'. It connotes disorder which is an unruly behavior unbecoming of an honorable man. So, *"do not abandon your position"* (NASB) especially when you are in the right. But when you are in the wrong, do not *"[show a resisting spirit]; for gentleness and calmness prevent or put a stop to great offences"* (AMP). In any case, the general admonition is that you do not quit or abandon your right just because a ruler is angry. The bottom-line: DO NOT PANIC!

Most times, politicians use street urchins, social miscreants and thugs to cause an uproar in the community in order to cause panic among the people. Why? So that they, the politicians, could start appealing for calm. This is to draw the attention of the people to themselves and make the people recognize them, acknowledge their "effort" at suing for peace. Their ultimate and often hidden agenda is that when election time approaches, they present themselves as the long-awaited messiahs of the land.

You should always remember as the saying goes, there is no smoke without a fire. And if there is a fire, someone kindled it. Men in the corridors of power do not want the citizens to realize that the real power of the state resides with and rests on them, the citizens. They do not want to leave the corridors of power but tightly hold on to it as if they are the only ones with working brains for leadership. So they devise and deploy any tools such as raising panic to divert the attention of the common man from that realization and knowledge of who really is the boss.

They stir the dust of panic such that the citizens lose focus on what is important and channel and expend their energy and scarce resources on dealing with the trending non issues. And this has been working well for the politicians but against us. That is why the citizens must learn to be calm in the face of some issues so they can carefully calculate before commenting on them. We must probe before participating and investigate before involving ourselves as well as investing our scarce resources in these issues.

The average citizen should know as matter of fact that the politicians are not the government, we are.

Yes, we are the government! Therefore, whenever the executive, the legislature or the judiciary – those representing us – make any attempt to raise the dust of fear and at using panic to divide us, and to stampede us into uninformed decisions and hurried conclusions, we must be armed with this information that we are the government. This is what I am revealing to us in this book. Hence, do not panic, do not leave your position and do not quit being in control until victory is assured.

LACK OF INTELLIGENCE

One of the major handicaps of our leaders across board is lack of intelligence. Now, someone might want to disagree with me, but before you do, let us look at what intelligence is from God's record and divine perspective. For that is the most authentic record of facts, figures, definitions and affirmations.

First, the wisest man, Solomon David of Israel advised, ***"Wisdom is the principal thing; therefore get wisdom: and with all thy getting get understanding"*** (Proverbs 4:7). Two components of intelligence highlighted in those lines of history above are wisdom and understanding. The third is captured in the following text by the same author and leader, Solomon: *"It takes wisdom to build a house, and understanding to set it on a firm foundation; it takes <u>knowledge</u> to furnish its rooms with fine furniture and beautiful draperies"* (Proverbs 24:3-4 TM).

Knowledge is the third component of intelligence. Hence, wisdom, knowledge and understanding make up the complete pack of intelligence. And the possession of this complete pack by an individual is possible, but rare to see in most of those that walk the corridors of power in this part. As it is with the leaders, so with most of the followers especially those valued for wisdom, who, unfortunately, lack it.

When you listen to conversations in public places amongst the citizens on the street, you will marvel at their height of knowledge – pieces of facts and figures. They seem to know much about the polity, economy and trending issues in the nation. They read a lot from the newspapers and magazines, get so much information from news on television and online platforms including the social media. Yet, their reactions and responses most of the time reveal lack of intelligence.

It is true that knowledge is power and information is vital for making quality decision. However, the task lies in making that quality decision which is only guaranteed by intelligence. Action that is fruitful and result-based is the attestation of one's possession of the complete pack of intelligence. A man of knowledge may still fail if he lacks the wisdom to manage and creatively use what he knows to produce result. A man of wisdom may still fail if he lacks information of what is going on in the city. That means he lacks one of the basic components of intelligence. Compare and contrast these lines of history:

"One day as I was observing how wisdom fare on this earth, I saw something that made me sit up and take notice. There was a small town with only a few people in it. A strong king came and mounted an attack, building trenches and attack posts around it. There was a poor but wise man in that town whose wisdom saved the town, but he was promptly forgotten. (He was only a poor man, after all.)" – Ecclesiastes 9:13-15 TM.

"One day when Jacob was cooking some stew, Esau arrived home from the wilderness exhausted and

hungry. Esau said to Jacob, "I'm starved! Give me some of that red stew... "All right," Jacob replied, "but trade me your rights as firstborn son." "Look, I'm dying of starvation!" said Esau. "What good is my birthright to me now?" "But Jacob said, "First you must swear that your birthright is mine." So Esau swore an oath, thereby selling all his rights as the firstborn to his brother, Jacob. Then Jacob gave Esau some bread and lentil stew. Esau ate the meal, then got up and left. He showed contempt for his rights as the firstborn." (Genesis 25:29-34 NLT).

My observation, analysis and submission of these two Bible history records will be based on the premise of wisdom, knowledge and understanding – intelligence.

The poor man in the Preacher's illustration has wisdom but lacks basic knowledge on creating wealth thus he is poor. While growing up in my town, I knew such men and women who were so full of wisdom that they were often invited by traditional rulers across the communities to mediate and settle conflicts and rifts amongst the people. They were wizards at that but were mostly poor, living in mud houses. Most of them had no formal education and were peasants all their lives. Except for few of them whose children were business men and lived averagely comfortable lives in the city, others lived and died in poverty and wretchedness.

Just like the poor but wise man in President Solomon's story, they stood up or the community but were never celebrated like their rich counterparts. Solomon remarked that ***"no man [seriously] remembered that poor man"*** (AMP). He followed it with a shocking truth or reality which saddens poor people but should provide a piece of vital information to them: ***"So even though wisdom is better than strength, those who are wise will be despised if they are poor. What they say will not be appreciated for long"*** (vs. 16 NLT).

Does it marvel you that the political elites in our land do anything including looting the nation's treasury, evading tax, and laundering money in order to remain relevant? Does it marvel you that the masses of this state who form a larger percentage of the poor populace will always be relegated to the rear? Even though some of our masses have the brains to turn the tides in this country, they would not be considered fit and qualified to run things as long as they are poor. But the real question is: Why is the bulk of the citizenry poor even with their evident wisdom? The answer can be traced to lack of intelligence.

I want to explore this argument further. The character in the second story, Esau, was a man of knowledge and strength. He was a hunter who also knew how to make his favorite red stew. But fateful day, he displayed a shallow level of understanding and poor sense of the value of his birthright. Simply put: He lacked wisdom and understanding.

Now, this is the major plague devastating the majority of the African people who truly are the government. They know a lot but show so little. They seldom ask relevant questions but argue about irrelevant issues. Meanwhile, those servants they send on errand at the local, state and federal government levels hijack the reins of authority, and begin to manipulate their destinies. Like Solomon lamented, this is a piece of bad business that goes on in this God-blessed republic and even in Africa. And I feel so pained in my heart.

Now to my conclusion on this point in this chapter, it would not be fair if I do not explain a little further what intelligence can really do to a people. Solomon noted in Proverbs 24:5-6, *"It's better to be wise than strong; intelligence outranks muscle any day. Strategic planning is the key to warfare; to win, you need a lot of good counsel."* (The Message, TM).

In this line, comparison is made between intelligence and physical strength which muscle represents. However, to win any battle, one needs brainpower and manpower. Brainpower has to do with wisdom, knowledge and understanding while manpower talks about muscle and numbers. And if we analyses further, the common man has advantage in numbers and muscles, while the few in the ruling class are privileged to have brainpower. And since a man of intelligence is ranked above a man with muscle, this switch became possible in our dear land.

Until the people of this country begin to seek wisdom, knowledge and understanding, which are compulsory leverages and mandatory joker to reclaim their position, this error will continue for a longer time. Oh yes, until we show that we know, this lopsided and artificial arrangement where slaves rule and princes ruin will continue for a long time. So, fellow citizens, open your eyes; awake from sleep and slumber, and balance the equation to reclaim your position. It is a mission that is possible.

LAZINESS

The last factor that is responsible for the switch I want us to discuss is laziness. The disinclination to exertion, unwillingness to engage in serious work, and the over-relaxed or leisurely disposition of the citizenry can all be used to describe or define laziness. When you ask a common man on the street what he thinks of the ugly trends in the country, and his reply is that he only cares about the food on his table, such a fellow is a typical indolent person. The opposite of indolence is industrious, and although many are industrious in their career or profession, they are indolent in weightier matters that decide their future in the country.

In verse fifteen of Ecclesiastes chapter ten, President Solomon made a striking observation about people valued for wisdom, but who unfortunately live the opposite or the contrast. It reads:

"The labor of fools wearies every one of them, because [he is so ignorant of the ordinary matters that] he does not even know how to get to town" (AMP).

The New Living Translation puts it this way: "Fools are so exhausted by a little work that they can't even (are too lazy to) find their way home" (Emphasis mine).

Again, as it is with the servants-turned-masters, so it is with the masters-turned-servants. Laziness is the bane of our country's advancement. Let me quote the same text from The Living Bible translation: ***"A fool is so upset by a little work that he has no strength for the simplest matter."*** What is this simplest matter? I will highlight it.

The simplest matter this history was talking about is the state of the nation. From the Amplified version of the Holy Bible, I will give the highlights. The state of the nation which comprises the governance of the state, the management of national resources, the recovery of our lost customary values, and the rebuilding of our mutual love for one another. These are issues or components of the simplest matter according to the wisest president. To a man of wisdom and intelligence, they are issues that he should be involved in. To a man of industry in both his personal career and national concerns, they are issues that he should get involved with. But to a lazy citizen, these matters are undesirable and unattainable.

The common man on whose shoulder rests the government of the nation as it were; who should engage all neighbors, public servants, and leaders of thoughts at all levels in constructive debate goes about crying like a hungry child. Those who should initiate debates on rejigging the economy, streamlining our cultures, restructuring the polity, and resuscitating the dying confidence of fellow citizens go about whining and complaining, murmuring and grumbling. They end up not doing anything to help but, rather, are filled with indolence and ineptitude. At the end, he complains that he is suffering. A poor man is always hungry in a feast! Why? Because he is lazy, redundant, and apathetically confused.

Civil servants have become civil lords because the bulk of the citizens are too lazy to demand accountability from them. Learned fellows have become learned failures because the self-acclaimed educated class are too lazy to hold them responsible for the obvious inanities compassing and emanating from the judiciary. Governors and legislators are swimming in murderous misappropriations of public funds with unrepentant impunity without a radical confrontation because the people nature has endowed with such responsibility have negligently refused to do the needful. Lazy folks all over the land! And Solomon lamented: ***"Laziness lets the roof leak, and soon the rafters begin to rot"*** (10:18 TLB).

It is widely believed and in most cases reported in the media that Nigerians are among the hardest working people in the world. It seems so, but I differ in my opinion. Truth is Nigerians are hard-working but far from being among the "most hard-working" people on earth. We can say so of most Nigerians in Europe, Asia and America but not those in Africa. Most of these so-called hard-working people are simply busy people – full of activity without accomplishment. This is especially the case with Nigerians in Nigeria and Africa.

Only a fraction of those in diaspora have actually distinguished themselves through hard work and commitment to their calling. The larger percentage of the populace are, at best, "hustlers" as they claim. If someone thinks that I am being unfair in my submission, please, take a look at available statistics. Of course, not the statistics provided by our government agencies or departments, but by some other independent firms.

Compare our country with Asian countries like Singapore, Malaysia, China, Indonesia, South Korea or even India, one can see the disparity in accomplishment which is the attestation to my submission. When you look at what they have achieved in few years and how we have remained almost stagnant in terms of technology, scientific discovery, economic and political stability, would you say that we are really working hard? Where is the evidence of our hard work?

Take a tour of the research centers across the country, they are shadows of reality. Where are our professors and academics? Take a survey of our airports, seaports, academic institutions, tourist centers and parks, museums and national monuments, you would smell the rottenness of neglect orchestrated by the redundancy of the people. President Solomon the wisest wrote:

"One day I walked by the field of an old lazybones, and then passed the vineyard of a lout; they were overgrown with weeds, thick with thistles, all the fences broken down. I took a long look and pondered what I saw; the fields preached me a sermon and I listened: 'A nap here, a nap there, a day off here, a day off there, sit back, take it easy – do you know what comes next? Just this: you can look forward to a dirt-poor life, with poverty as your permanent houseguest!" (Proverbs 24:30-34 TM).

We are still looking at laziness among the rank and file of the citizenry, with emphasis on the average citizen, not basically those in the corridors of political power. We will discuss the indolence among the political and religious class later in this book. Why we must critically discuss this factor that is eating up the common man is because it is one of the major facilitators of the switch we are addressing here.

These people plant, (initiate and invent ideas) but they do not tend their garden (work on the initiatives or ideas) to ensure fruit is produced. They, sometimes, spot what is wrong in the leadership of the state, but do nothing more than sit back and look on. Some of them make some bold moves by organizing protests, but at the end, the heat dies down and almost nothing comes out of it. The mission sometimes gets aborted by counter protests or the organizers are "settled" with *Greek gift* and the objective is defeated. They do not last through because they are apathetic and faint even before they arrive their destination.

In other instances, most of them do not want to stick out their neck in defense of their constitutional rights. At the slightest resistance or opposition from those they elected to represent them, they waver and quiver, shake and quake, falter and fall. When there is little shaking in the economy, and these civil-servants-turned-lords announce it to the winds, you see these kings and nobles-turned-common people begin to cry out that they are marginalized or neglected. And because they are lazy and weak to think out of the box for solutions, they begin to cry for help as if the world would end at that time. Then, their servants – civil, public, or whatever – would seize the moment to further enslave them. What an error! Slaves ruling sons; princes bowing to peasants! I weep!

So if you ask me again, I would tell you again that we are a lazy people. The only hard work we are champions at is celebrating emptiness, mediocrity and incompetence. Someone wins election by fraud, and we know it, they roll out drum and we join to celebrate him. Our uncles and kinsmen return home with looted funds, we organize social spree to celebrate them. Most times, a thanksgiving service is held in our churches to thank God for their breakthroughs.

Why do we celebrate them? Because we do not appreciate harvest from hard-work, or promotion by merit, or riches by righteousness. This is because our values – the values we inherited from the bulk of our pre-colonial ancestry – have been grossly eroded and brushed aside in our pursuit for vanity. We give up on the most essentials and embark on a wild goose chase to fill the emptiness and vacuum created by greed, ungodly covetousness, and cravings for the forbidden.

Why would someone with complete hands and legs become an armed robber or pen-robber? Why would someone cheat in an examination or even defraud others? Simply put: Laziness! They do not use their common sense to reason that the amount of energy they channel into robbery, looting or ritual killing, is the same to do honest work and earn decent and honest wages. They steal, rob, loot and kill because they want to avoid the labor of real, honest work.

And when those in authority see this among our people, they throw crumbs from the stolen wealth to us, and out of laziness, we scramble with one another for the crumbs. And they continue to sit tight while we groan and moan and gnash our teeth in poverty when the crumbs do not satisfy us. But I pray that this error will be corrected, and the order where slaves rule over sons will be reversed once and for all.

Chapter Five

STRIKING A BALANCE

There is a saying that what is good for the goose is good for the gander. To balance a mathematical equation especially in algebraic equations, what is done to the left is often done to the right. That is to say that addition and subtraction, multiplication and division become vital in striking a balance in our over-heated systems and lopsided structures.

There is a growing concern in the nation. Amidst several agitations and clarion calls for the restructuring of the nation, most schools of thoughts believe that unless a drastic move by major stakeholders to straighten out the crooked legacies that have begrimed our souls is taken as soon as possible, the very collapse of the foundation of our collective existence as One Nigeria is predictable.

There is also an increased consciousness of the reality of the gross incompetence of actors on the political and economic stage, the painful ineffectiveness of government manifestoes and policies, as well as the unimaginable inconsistency in leadership prognosis. All these have been responsible for all sorts of disturbances in the society. These disturbances, which are quite unnecessary and preventable, keep sweeping across our lands, resurfacing and resurging with untamed momentum despite constant calls by well-meaning countrymen – technocrats and democrats, academics and other professionals – for calm and repose.

But instead of calm, what we have is chaos. Instead of repose, we have seen more rebellion. The serious challenge posed by this debacle has been the inability of major stakeholders and opinion leaders to see the crass imbalance of the present political and socio-economic structures of our nation. Not only do they fail to see the imbalance, but the urgent need to strike an acceptable balance that would kick-start the processes for national growth and development.

In this chapter, I will try to highlight areas of this erroneous imbalance as well as prescribe and proffer time-tested scripture-based corrections. It is instructive that we also assay the damage done by this unjust order and then get ready to sail to a new level of sanity in our system.

The wisest president, Solomon, who made these striking observations from years of study, research and experiential discovery on the seat or saddle of his country's prime leadership left no one in doubt what trouble they could cause for any nation if left unaddressed and unattended to. So, I will not have done a good job if I overlook these grey areas that should compulsorily receive good attention. The reason is that they are responsible for our nation's quagmire and hunting quandaries.

Areas of Erroneous Imbalance

Immaturity Given a Place of Prominence

"Here's a piece of bad business I've seen on this earth (Africa), an error that can be blamed on whoever is in charge: Immaturity is given a place of prominence…" (Ecclesiastes 10:5 TM, emphasis mine). One of the many ill-characteristics of a slave is immaturity. Most of the people that occupy the saddle in our land are unripe and not fully developed for the job of leadership. Some of them act like kindergarten, nay, over-pampered kindergarten who were wrongly given the privilege to ascend the throne. They are schooled, no doubt, but are seldom educated in sound knowledge, ethics and etiquettes that behoove the exalted offices they occupy. That is why they behave childishly even in places like the hallowed chambers and sacred quarters.

The immaturity of a slave in a place of prominence is more pronounced in relation to how they handle state affairs or run the economy of the organization, local council area, community or country. Their decisions and policies are both foolish and selfish because they are wearied by the noble task of sound education and study such that they do not even know how to get things properly done. The Preacher corroborates this: *"The labor of fools wearies every one of them, because [he is so ignorant of the ordinary matters that] he does not even know how to get to town"* (10:15 AMP). This is a big problem!

A careful study of our civil service would make one cry for our country. Long before I began to follow the trending matters and news in the land, I had heard a lot about this unfortunate scenario. It is a case where unqualified people are hired for plum jobs in key sectors of our economy, not on merit, but on sentiment. If the director of a particular government agency is from a particular tribe, he quickly favors people from his tribe even when others from the other tribes are more qualified for the work. When there are contracts to be awarded, he considers people from his ethnic group, political party, religious group, or social class first even if they do not merit it based on requisite qualifications. At the end, the system is compromised and progress is stalled or stiffened, which facilitates poor output and diminished revenue.

Read this: *"Jeroboam now built the city of Shechem in the hill country of Ephraim, and it became his capital. Later he built Peniel. Jeroboam thought, "Unless I'm careful, the people will want a descendant of David as their king. When they go to Jerusalem to offer sacrifices at the Temple, they will become friendly with King Rehoboam; then they will kill me and ask him to be their king instead." So on the advice of his counsellors, the king had two golden calf idols made and told the people, "It's too much trouble to go to Jerusalem to worship; from now on these will be your gods – they rescued you from your captivity in Egypt!" ... He also made shrines on the hills and ordained priests from the rank and file of the people – even those who were not from the priestly tribe of Levi"* (1 Kings 12:25-32 TLB).

When immaturity is given a place of prominence, the "lucky" few, out of foolishness, hijack a smooth-running system and plunges it into a pit of impoverishment. And because they do not know how to get things done, they trade blames, push responsibilities through their rank and file, and avoid to accept that they lack the basics to make things work for good.

Another translation puts that piece of Bible history thus: *"...when they give great authority to foolish people..."* (NLT). When foolish people are given great authority is like when a slave is made ruler over a prince. Proverbs 19:10 says, *"It doesn't seem right for a fool to succeed or for a slave to rule over princes!"* This is because fools make promises they cannot keep. They tell the people from whom they hijack the reins of power that they will treat all fair and square. But at the end, they discard those promises as necessary ploy to woo them and be in charge.

Now, you ask, why do they do that? Answer: They are foolish, immature, unripe and undeveloped for the task which they promised to deliver. Bible history agrees: ***"It is foolish and rash to make a promise to the Lord*** (or the people) ***before counting the cost"*** (Proverbs 20:25 TLB, emphasis mine).

Immaturity of those in authority has caused this nation of ours monumental loss and grievous moments. Promises are made during election campaigns, but they are not fulfilled because they are largely made out of ignorance, deception, and desperation to be on the saddle. Our economy is the largest in Africa yet the citizenry groan and moan in utter hardship because those saddled with the responsibility of wealth distribution are immature and selfish.

When foolish and immature people are given great authority, abuse and impunity ascend the throne and thrive at the expense of the people's happiness. When foolish and immature people are given a position of prominence either by error or act of terror, the laws are misinterpreted and biased judgment proceed from the law courts. The list is endless! This imbalance must be set right for things to go the way they should in a healthy society.

People of Proven Worth Are Given Low Positions

This is another problem in our nation. It is no longer news that our economic and political space are in great danger. This is because those who are managing it are not the right people. Those who could manage the economy and polity more efficiently are deserting this country in droves. This is what is referred to as brain drain. History reveals that this expression was first coined in London to describe the outflow of scientists and technologists to the United States of America and Canada in the early 1950s.

And what is brain drain? It is the migration of educated or talented people from less economically advanced cities to more economically advanced cities or towns. Careful study has shown that a large number of Nigerian medical professionals practice in the United States, Canada and India. In fact, it is also an established fact that there seems to be more qualified and well-read medical minds outside the country than there are presently in the country.

Most of the people that are contributing greatly to the advancement of these other countries left our countries because they were not considered fit for those offices that are now mostly occupied by quacks. So, you see that the result of giving low positions to men of proven worth is that they reject it, run to other places where they are celebrated thus making way for upstarts to run the show. This is a terrible imbalance in our structure and system.

President Solomon lamented that it was a piece of bad business he saw in his time. Need I say that this situation is now worse in our clime? A situation where maturity is made to take a back seat while immaturity is given prominence is not only a bad business, but a highly lamentable, regrettable and condemnable development. Nothing kills and destroys a nation faster. A country where people with great ideas are side-lined cannot produce a creative atmosphere for positivity. Thus, the dream of progress and prosperity will always, if not eternally elude such a nation.

When God was about moving the people and nation of Israel into the Promised Land, He instructed Moses their prime minister to send some officials to spy or scout out the country. He was to appoint credible people – the qualified leaders from the twelve tribes. God said: *"...Send one man from each tribe, each one a tried-and-true leader in the tribe"* (Numbers 13:2 TM).

This account is true and remains the standard for every organization, administration or country especially in a representative government as ours. The Word of God is the standard and forms the template for quality governance and good living. Any leader or organization that must thrive and succeed must consult the Word of God and choose His template for a smooth-run system. God has always maintained this standard and human beings made in His image should adopt it in order to live a good life. But unfortunately, that has not been the case in my country.

Our leaders have often neglected the standard set by God or treated it with contempt or at best, regarded it as meant for "Church people". They have always designed theirs which has brought no small disappointment to the nation and her people. When God gave Moses that command, He was not giving it to the church, but to a nation. The selection was not going to come from church, and so that command has nothing to do with the church. It was a national mandate, not a religious thing!

Apart from experiencing this awful brain drain, relegating bright minds to the backseat has other dire consequences. It promotes anarchy and disregard for the rule of law. It also results in rebellion and encourages criminal tendencies and activities amongst the citizenry. Cases of people of proven worth and obvious ingenuity in low positions who become a nuisance to the system abound in this land.

When those who should be subordinates and assistants are put in charge of managing key public offices or agencies, the most qualified people who are placed under are pushed into devising ways to make up for their "loss" and denial. This has been the major cause if inefficiency in our civil service. Since the bright minds are made to take lower positions, their level of dedication to service and height of patriotism drop; redundancy sets in, and the agency or commission suffers. The Nigeria Civil Service is awash with this notorious imbalance such that the nation is robbed of growth and advancement.

Take for instance our system where men and women who head our ministries, departments and agencies are either brothers, sisters, cousins, uncles, aunties, or even children and buddies of those in power, with the country neither advancing nor accomplishing much. Then, you ask: Where are the men of Issachar? Where are the daughters of Zelophehad?

The Book of Chronicles has a record of the men of Issachar whose leaders or chiefs were just 200 in number, yet all Israel were at their command. 1 Chronicles 12:32). History credited them with having *"knowledge of what Israel should do"* (NASB). Yes, they were just *"200 leaders of the tribe…men (who) understood the signs of the time and know the best course for Israel to take"* (NLT). It did not happen in Mars or the Moon; it happened here on earth – in Israel. President David discovered these men and welcomed them into his administration, and the result was the huge success he recorded in life and career. But sadly, it is not so in my country. That is why people are crying for change in the era of so-called change!

Fellow citizens, we must go back to the design room, pick up the drawing board, and redesign what we have at the moment, which can be best described in the words of Honorable Patrick Obahiagbon as *cabalocracy* – the government of the cabals, by the cabals, and for the cabals! This is a robbery of true democracy! Until we do this; confront and correct this daylight robbery of the fundamental rights of the qualified citizens, our dear country will ever remain a joke.

Slaves Riding on Horses

"It isn't right for a fool to live in luxury or for a slave to rule over princes!" (Proverbs 19:10 NLT). The observation of the wisest president, Solomon David, in this piece of history is quite striking and revealing. Our society is filled with different kinds of people including those who claim to be timbres and calibers, *irokos* and mahoganies, etc. The sad truth remains that some of these people are simply slaves riding on horses.

When I was in the senior high school in the early 90s, there was a class mate of mine who was very fair in complexion. So, as a result of his very light skin, one of our teachers nicknamed him 'Unfortunate European'. Most of the time, he would smile whenever the teacher addressed him by that name. At other times, he would frown especially when we, his classmates called him the name. But one discovery I made while we were passing out from that school in 1992 was that he had a secret liking for that name.

You know, to think that he was being acknowledged as a European although born and raised by African parents who never went anywhere near an airport let alone living in Europe gave him a kind of feeling of respect. He probably had this feeling of not being "African" among those often seen as "these blacks". But I knew his problem: he did not actually understand the full meaning of the word "unfortunate" at that time. That feeling of being European without the comprehension of the word "unfortunate" can be likened to a slave riding on a horseback. This analogy best suits some men in power in this clime.

The problem with this kind of imbalance is that it paints a very poor and negative picture of the state of the nation. When slaves are riding on horses, it leaves the nation much to be desired. It forms a strong opinion on intelligent minds that the situation is the best the nation can produce. Thus, it either shuts out noble men or forces others to look for where else to rule and reign. This is one major reason why people of great intellectual base are not eager to declare for the throne. They become weak-willed and apathetic.

Each time I read that line in President Solomon's treatise in Ecclesiastes, the first question that pops up in my mind is: Where did the slaves get the horses they ride on? Going by the definition of a slave as a servant who is either owned or bought or hired to carry out his master's commands, how did he get the horse? One rationale is that he probably stole it from God-knows-where, brought it into his master's estate, and began to ride on it.

Another thought is that he probably killed his master and took over his estate and all that he owned. Thus, he made his master's progeny who were supposed to rule after their father as princes to take the position of slaves and servants. These probabilities are actually realities during the era of kings in Israel and Judah. Read the Bible for yourself and you will agree with me. This scenario worries me seriously.

When we look around and see this imbalance play out and go as if it is our heritage, one cannot help but wonders what the future holds for our dear country. Slaves riding on horses in any society should naturally worry any concerned, patriotic citizen. It is absurd, abnormal, and outrageously atrocious! This is because according to our most excellent scholar, poet, and administrator of international repute, President Solomon, *"Luxury is not fitting for a fool; much less for a slave to rule over princes"* (NASB).

If you followed me from the beginning of this book, I stated the characteristics of slaves. One is that they are not wise and intelligent, hence, cannot efficiently manage resources. They are wasteful, unjustly extravagant, and prodigal in handling state affairs. That is what makes them slaves in the first place. So, when they find their way to the top through hook or crook, they exhibit slave mentality, indulge in irregularity, exude social impurity and display executive malfeasance with untamed impunity. They believe that the rightful owners might arise any time and reclaim their position. This is usually the worst nightmare of slaves.

The thought of losing the stolen or hijacked horse and thus returning to their original position hunts them. They cannot imagine returning to a state of irrelevance and insignificance in the society. This is a major reason they do everything inhumanely possible to cling to the saddle. They love the seat just like the Pharisees of Jesus' day loved the uppermost seats at feasts and hailing in public places. This is the plague of our time, devastating the economy, rubbishing our international image and polluting our spiritual space. Probe and pry into every sector of this country, you will see slaves riding on horses. Too bad! But let us take it further.

When slaves ride on horses, many things go wrong. History is replete with many instances of this ugly scene. However, I will highlight just a few for convenience sake.

The People Groan and Sigh

"When the [uncompromisingly] righteous are in authority, the people rejoice; but when the wicked (<u>compromisingly unrighteous</u>) man rules, the people groan and sigh" (Proverbs 29:2 AMP) Emphasis mine.

This is one of the outcomes when slaves who find their way through whatever means to the seat of authority ride on horses. We all know that slaves do not have honor; they do not appreciate self-esteem. They believe that opportunity comes but once, even though that is not entirely true. So informed by their lack of nobility and the understanding of the rule for godly living, they treat those they manage to rule like slaves.

It is a natural tendency, and sadly, a very high tendency for people who have been subjected to some form of servitude to have the strong belief that everyone else should go through the same experience. God knew this and strongly commanded Israel through Moses not to make life hard for their servants, reminding them that they were slaves in Egypt – Deuteronomy 24:14-15, 17-22. Without that commandment, I believe the people of Israel would have treated their servants the way the Egyptians treated them. That would have resulted in groaning and sighing.

So, the Israelites followed God, the God of their fathers. But the slaves we have on this side of the globe are not so. These are servants who have turned themselves into small and silly lords. Men who hijacked the running of the system by crook, and have continuously displayed foolishness, refusing to lose their ungodly grip on the saddle. Instead, they have subjected the unlucky people under their influence to a life of rigor and reproach. One thing I know and persuaded of is that their time is fast running out and the original inheritors of the throne will mount it soon.

The Nobles Are Hunted Down

There is a record in 2 Kings 11:1-3 about an incident among the royal class in old Israel. It reads: *"Athaliah was the mother of Ahaziah. When she saw that her son was dead, she took over. She began by massacring the entire royal family. But Jehosheba, daughter of King Joram and sister of Ahaziah, took Ahaziah's son Joash and kidnapped him from among the king's sons slated for slaughter. She hid him and his nurse in a private room away from Athaliah. He didn't get killed. He was there with her, hidden away for six years in the Temple of God. Athaliah, oblivious to his existence, ruled the country"* (The Message).

Slaves always stay alert and pray for such ungodly opportunity so they can mount the throne. While their masters are alive and well, they remain quiet, not humble; calm and calculating, strategizing what to do when their masters make a grave mistake or are dead. Remember what President Solomon said,

"There is another evil I have seen under the sun. Kings and rulers make a grave mistake when they give great authority to foolish people…" (NLT).

So, when this scenario takes place or plays out, and the slaves hijack the throne, they begin to hunt down men and women of honor, self-esteem, noble background, and all those who would oppose their slave rule. That was what this evil mother of Mr. President did immediately her son was gunned down in a political battle with General Jehu. History recorded that *"she took over"* and *"ruled the country"* (vs. 3). Are you surprised?

When men of intelligence come out and reveal to us that there are cabals running the country from the presidency to the legislature to the judiciary, you had better believe them. When our first lady spoke out in overseas during an interview that her husband, our president, was not the one in charge, but cabals, some people called her names. But history is not silent about these things. It happened in Israel. It is happening in Nigeria and maybe other countries of Africa and the world too.

So, the first national project this evil woman, who had been one of the cabals but maybe not in the good books of her son, the president, embarked on was the slaughter of her own grandsons. Why? So that none of them would mount the throne; so that she could rule the country, because that had been her ambition all the while. That is the first thing slaves think of doing – destroying what might pose a threat to their ungodly ambition of taking over the horse to ride on. She then plunged the entire country into fear and there was panic amongst concerned citizens and stakeholders.

But thank God for few men who knew their purpose in the country. Ably led by a very brave priest named Jehoiada, they organized themselves and restored the country's polity to order. In all honesty, we need brave men like those priests in our country. Men who would not be swayed by the rising profiles of the cabals or intimidated by the propaganda of their protégé. We need such men in our land who would summon steel courage to refuse bribes and settlements and legitimately carry out the divine assignment of ridding the land of slaves in places of authority. Jehoiada and his men did it in old Israel and there was jubilation once again in the land. This is what must happen in this country and in the African continent. Take this as a prophecy: It will happen in no distant time.

Redemption of the Nation is Far-to-Fetch

Another worrisome thing that happens when slaves ride on horses is that the nation goes from good to bad and from bad to worse. President Solomon says, *"What sorrow for the land ruled by a servant, the land whose leaders feast in the morning"* (Ecclesiastes 10:16 NLT). When slaves rule, the nation goes to ruins! This is typical of some countries of the Third World. African countries are worse hit by this plague.

When you pitch the state of the nations in Africa against the enormous human and natural resources found in them, you naturally but truthfully come to the conclusion that those in power are no more than slaves and unprofitable servants.

I have stated here earlier that slaves do not have the capacity to manage resources well; they squander wealth. So, to have them in the corridors of power or seat of authority is a tragedy which spells doom for any nation. Yes, it is a tragedy for any country that is suffering economic setback to now, by mistake or error, enthrone slaves or unprofitable servants as their leaders. If there was any hope of resurrection of such ailing economy before these slaves ascend the throne, that hope is quickly extinguished by their callousness, high-handedness, and inexperience.

Honestly, it is not in slaves to redeem a nation. It is not in their character so counting on them is like expecting hell to freeze or cocks to grow teeth. Impossible! It is the work of noblemen to resurrect an ailing economy and make it grow and flourish.

Ecclesiastes laments: ***"Woe to you, O land, when your king is a child or a servant and when your officials feast in the morning!"*** What happens when a man feasts in the morning is that he gets drunk and over-eaten and neglects his duties for the day. When leaders feast in the morning, they lose their sense of service and responsibility, accountability and direction. They usually sleep off, forgetting that there is work to be done. How then can they focus on measures to pull their countries out of recession? How can they build sustainable structures for national development?

No nation ruled by unprofitable servants can be prosperous. Redemption of such a nation from hardship and slavery is highly elusive and unpredictable because slaves do not think or worry about the redemption of the people or the land. All they think and worry about is their own redemption which they do not see as intertwined with that of the nation. And since they find a horse to ride on, what occupies their mind is to keep a firm grip on it so as to keep riding on it.

There is a Collapse of State Affairs

When slaves rule, there is a collapse of state affairs. President Solomon added that as a result of this seriously disappointing imbalance, *"...the rafters [of state affairs] decay..."* (Ecclesiastes 10:18 AMP). No sector of the country seems to be working perfectly in order at the moment. The truth is that no sector of a country works progressively with slaves riding on horsebacks. This is because they are lazy, indolent, unproductive and nonchalant in their response to national issues.

You know, they want to take life easy and enjoy the cruise while it lasts. Like I said earlier, they know that such opportunities necessitated by the mistake of the people do not always come around. Therefore, they indulge in easy-life, putting aside the urgent need to fix the country and embark on a wild goose chase. The wisest president that ever walked this earth observed that *"[instead of repairing the breaches, the officials] make a feast for laughter, serve wine to cheer life, and [depend on tax] money to answer for all of it"* (vs. 19 AMP). Can you see that? It is only a slave that drinks to forget the pains of responsibility. He sees hard work as unnecessary punishment, not as a necessary ingredient for success and a good life.

The question he asks himself is: Why should I work again when I have the nation's treasury at my beck and call? He simply concludes that it is no use trying to make the system work which could bring out the best in the people. What is his fear? The people might become aware and fully conscious of their rights to the throne and commence the process to remove him. This is his greatest fear; his most worrisome nightmare – the people.

That is why they use all manner of methods to cause distractions and diversions in the country. Their goal or objective is to engage the people with unnecessary debates and gossips on non-issues to divert their attention away from the core, real issues. And most times, the people fall for their gimmicks while the state continues to collapse into further doldrums and darkness.

This horrible state of collapse of state affairs is an attestation to the unintelligent nature of these slaves. They try to approach every challenge of the state with same solution that has failed to produce national success in the time of their predecessors. Being unintelligent, they do not use their brains. That is why Solomon observed: *"Remember: The duller the ax, the harder the work."* Then he advised, *"Use your head: The more brains, the less muscles"* (Ecclesiastes 10 vs. 10 TM). But slaves do not understand this. Too bad!

Now, having highlighted these imbalances, how do we correct them? First, we must start from the foundation. The foundation of the problem should be fundamentally addressed. One of the greatest poets and psalmist, David, noted: ***"The foundation of law and order have collapsed. What can the righteous do?"*** (Psalm 11:3 NLT). That is to say that if the foundations of the society – education, governance, religion, law, etc. – collapse, the right-thinking people will have a Herculean task fixing the society.

Howbeit, there is hope. That hope lies in the hands of godly people who should rise to the challenge. Yes, only the unyieldingly and uncompromisingly righteous people can salvage the nation by rebuilding the broken or crooked foundation. It is only when the righteous rise to the occasion would the community be rid of bad eggs. Our most reliable Bible History buttressed: ***"When right-living people bless the city, it flourishes..."*** (Proverbs 11:11 TM). That is it!

Why does an error often seem to become a tradition in a society? Why does it appear that the best that can rule a nation as ours is a bunch of incompetent folks?

Why do we have more evil-minded people in positions of influence in all tiers of government in the country? The simple answer is: Good men do not rise to do the needful. They have become so passive, dull and docile, being inundated with the erroneous belief that quietness means humility. Farce! Quietness never means humility.

There are so many people who are quiet and easy-going but are full of pride and arrogance. What they possess is false humility. When good men with balanced intellectual capacities and healthy rationale fold their arms and expect God to send angels to run the nation, men and women – slaves – who have lost sparkle and elasticity seize the saddle and spoil things. That is the problem; that is where it lies.

Good men must visit the foundation of the society and repair the breaches. When the foundation is fixed, the entire structure of the society will then have strong pivot to keep the balance. Thus, no matter the force that comes to shake the structure, it would not be pushed down. This is because the foundation is strong, solid and secure. The foundation of Nigeria and many other African countries need urgent repair.

There is need to address the root in order to get the real cure of our maladies. This exercise is mandatory to achieving any agenda of restructuring of the nation and the continent. I will talk more about this in the next chapter which is the last chapter of this book. This book will not be complete without adequately, to an appreciable extent, talking about more solutions in balancing the imbalances that have been identified in the treatise. This is my usual way of closing my books – with my final perspectives on the subject matter.

Chapter six

FINAL PERSPECTIVES

Basically, this is where I tend to be myself; to say things the way I see and understand them. I tend to be more open-minded, more evasive, and often times, I sound radical, nay, more radical to some folks. But to me and to some dynamic minds like me, it does not really matter. What is more important is if my musings are reasonable, positively convincing and relevant to the pursuance of truth. If my arguments and submissions appeal to the intellect and intelligence of men of understanding; if they are based on strong evidence and forcefully persuasive to clear heads and clean hearts, then I will go on and spit them out, notwithstanding.

First, let me traditionally appreciate your level of tolerance in assimilating the hard truths coated with no-sweet flavors in the chapters before this last one. And that is, if you truly devoted time to go through the pages. Yes, you are highly appreciated from my end, and, Thank you, again. Most people do not have the stomach for the truth; they love a lie and live it.

This is especially the case with leaders, nay, slaves-turned-masters who fortunately find themselves in an environment where lies are trending and selling fast. Across our lands, in this part of civilization, many have been deceived to believe that truth does not sell, and therefore, should not be invested in. But I vehemently disagree with such outrageous rubbish because the just shall live by faith and truth!

Now back to the concrete matter. President Solomon, the author of Ecclesiastes wrote: *"Woe to you, O land, when your king is a child or a servant* (a slave) *and when your officials* (politicians, elder statesmen, etc.) *feast in the morning! Happy (fortunate and to be envied) are you, O land, when your king is a free man and of noble birth and character and when your officials feast at the proper time – for strength and not for drunkenness! Through indolence (laziness, idleness) the rafters [of state affairs] decay and the roof sinks in, and through idleness of the hands the house leaks. [Instead of repairing the breaches, the officials* (politicians, elder statesmen, etc.,)] *make a feast for laughter, serve wine to cheer life, and [depend on tax] money to answer for all of it"* (10:16-19 AMP, Emphasis mine).

Before I begin to give vent to my musings and sum up this book with the shots as I see them, we must note again that the above piece of beautiful history was the keen observation of the wisest man and leader, President or King Solomon. In fact, he was not just the wisest, but the wealthiest world leader, president and commander in chief of the armed forces of Israel of Bible days who dazzled the world with his brilliance. To see the detailed profile of this wise man as I insightfully captured it from Bible exposition, you need to read my book, **"Vanity Republic – The Errors of our Heroes Past Volume 5"** published in e-Book and paperback formats on www.amazon.com/kindlestore.

So, it was not an observation by a layman or a novice in state affairs, but one made out of experience from the seat of authority and backed with strong evidence of events and time of occurrence. He must have observed how kings of his time misruled their nations and they ended in disgrace and shame. History is replete with such examples. Even in our contemporary times, we can spot most leaders who fit into the picture Solomon painted with those scriptural lines centuries ago. Particularly in Africa, and most unfortunately in Nigeria the giant of Africa, this picture seems to be more glaring. So sad!

When we look at those lines President Solomon wrote, we will find that any country ruled by servants or slaves is in big trouble. *"Woe to you, O land..."* means that country is to be pitied; the land is doomed and finished! In such a land where the king – president, governor, councilor, director general, etc. – is a child or a servant or a slave, there would be more display of foolishness than wisdom. This is because Solomon also noted that foolishness is bound in the heart of a child! It means that such a president, governor or chairman is inexperienced, incompetent to judge right and inefficient to deliver the gains of good governance. This is why the country will be in a mess.

When people say there is a cabal ruling the country, it is an indication that the men and women who should pilot the affairs of the community, constituency or country have been "overthrown" by slaves. Every day in the news, the press reports either their findings, speculations or interviews conducted with some eminent personalities who reveal these things and that there have been a switch in the leadership of the nation.

Let me refresh your mind with the news of a certain first lady of my country who went gaga with the confession that a set of group of people widely acknowledged as cabals had hijacked the running of the country from her husband. To some, that was the confession of the decade or century that a first lady could summon such courage to expose the ills in her husband's government. But to me, it came as a different message: Slaves rule! It is a message which is corroborated by President Solomon's submission: *"Woe to you, O land, when your king is a child"*. I mean no insult to any leader, but in making my candid input by this means, I must state my convictions plainly and be truthful with my conscience and my country as possible as God has given me the ability and grace.

In fact, it is an insult and a grave error in a land like ours so blessed by God with men and women of intelligence and foresight to be reported as being ruled by cabals. Haba! It is an insult on all the countries of Africa that look unto us as their big brother. To me, it showed that either the people we elect into leadership positions are not capable of holding the fort or that they deceive us and betray the mandate once delivered to them. This is another error that must be corrected as quickly as possible.

Let me refer to this, and I think it is worthy of mention. When former President Goodluck Jonathan lost out in 2015 general elections, he was quoted as saying that Nigerians would miss him when he was long gone. This information was shared on his Facebook timeline at a time. At once, I sent him a personal message via the same platform, but commented on the post that "we" would not miss him.

As far as I am concerned, Mr. President is the number one citizen of the country with enormous powers and authority backed up by the sovereign constitution to make the country work. As the commander in chief of the armed forces, he is expected to have his officers and men under check and control of his leadership. So, if good governance is not attained in the country especially at the federal level; if the economy, polity, social service and structure as well as other sectors are not properly working, he takes the blame.

How can you be the commander in chief and yet be a puppet in the hands of slaves? How can you be the commander in chief and yet you are being commanded by men who cannot boldly show their faces to the country? They hide under your weak leadership to terrorize the entire country, and you want us to believe that you are the commander in chief? No! Not anymore in the new Nigeria that is just emerging. Things are going to be different henceforth. Mark my words and take them as prophecy.

The worst insult leaders can heap on their citizens is to show incompetence and weakness in piloting the nation and its affairs. And I submit that the people of this country have suffered it for so long. I feel sad and disappointed when I hear some people in positions of influence addressing some Nigerians like us as being insolent when they are the ones who have not only been insolent but abusive and callous.

You hand our beautiful country and collective patrimony to slaves who go in the name of cabals, and you have the effrontery to label us insolent. You display nonchalance and play Adam to our plight and pains, yet you point fingers accusing us of not being patriotic and loyal to our country. All the promises you and your political parties made during campaigns for elections never became actualized, and when we cry out, you say we are asking for too much. What an insult!

Is it not the fundamental right of a child to cry when he is hungry? Or should a hard worker not complain when he is not paid his wage? Citizens are on forced fasting while the cabals go on feasting. Woe to the country whose leaders and officials feast in the morning! Nigeria is seen as a country of 57 years old, and as such should be playing in the super league of advancement and development. This being so when placed side by side other nations of the same age, size and treasure base that are doing better in education, technology, science, economy and social services.

Even some African countries that cannot boast or brag about the kind and size of natural resources we are blessed with are living far above our standard. Our land is green but her people are dry and grey because our politicians, elder statesmen and other officials feast in the morning. So, for the rest of the day, week, month or years, the work remains undone.

Just consider the member of days our lawmakers spend sitting to discuss our policies and problems, and the days they spend in recess and on vacation. If any corporate organization operates like that, it will close down in matter of few years. Then, put that calculation in perspective of what they earn in salaries, allowances and other emoluments, you would agree with President Solomon that the country is in trouble.

It is true they earn these bogus pay-packets "legitimately" because they are being paid by the system. But the real argument is: Who pays them this outrageous sum? It is the system which is being sustained by the laws they make and run by men who manipulate the laws to favor their appointers. Why is this so? Simple: If these lawmakers are not well taken care of by those appointees, they would react and begin the process for either their recall or removal from office. And if the cabals try to oppose the payment of those outrageous sums, they would raise and move a motion to revisit the policies that make it possible for those cabals to hold sway. This is what President Solomon was saying when he pointed out that slaves ride on horsebacks due to the error that proceed from kings and leaders. (Ecclesiastes 10:5). *"Woe to the land whose leaders behave like children and feast in the morning!"* (vs. 16).

Consider again: Immediately our independence was granted and celebrated in 1960, a bunch of slaves revolted, fiercely and forcefully hijacked the system, and plunged our dear land into depression and darkness. One military coup after another, they buried our dignity, held us out to public ridicule and plundered our economy like raging and roving bandits who care less of the aftermath. They took our wealth overseas, helped in developing foreign lands, and came home to blame it on us. If they saw this country as theirs, they would not have so dealt with us.

But you know how they think, it is not in their character to be noble because they are not, in Solomon's words, *"of noble birth and character"*. They feast in the morning because they do not have the agenda to save their country from going under. They do not even believe that their country can go under because they still know some people will work to produce the oil and gas, to fuel their greed and fill their gluttony. That is why they are callous and corrupt. No wonder they are cabals!

But let us look and consider this too. Heaven gives the earth the kind of leaders it deserves. Scriptures say that as long as the heir remains a child, he will be under tutors and governors because he is no different from slaves! Why would a land be ruled by cabals, slaves and glorified servants? Listen: People get the leaders they ignorantly ask for.

The nation of Israel under Prophet Samuel asked for a king and God consented even though He felt that they rejected them. The truth is that a group of armed robbers would not elect a police man in active service as the patron or chairman of their association. So also, men of crooked conscience will not elect or appoint a preacher of righteousness as their advisor.

<u>Down the Blind Alley</u>

When a people forsake the source of clean water, they end with a stinking stream. Like I wrote in my book, **"Partisan Politics – The Errors of our Heroes Past, Volume Three"**, Nigeria is much like Israel of Bible times. We move with the winds of the time; we hardly stand for something concrete for so long.

Prophet Isaiah published or broadcasted a message from God to Israel during the presidency of Uzziah, Jotham, Ahaz, and Hezekiah – all of Judah.

"Heaven and earth, you're the jury. Listen to God's case: "I had children and raised them well, and they turned on me. The ox knows who's boss, the mule knows the hand that feeds him, but not Israel (Nigeria). *My people don't know up from down. Shame! Misguided God-dropouts, staggering under their guilt-baggage. Gang of miscreants* (cabals), *band of vandals* (looters) *– my people have walked out on me, their God…walked off and never looked back. Why bother even trying to do anything with you when you just keep to your bullheaded ways? You keep beating your heads against brick walls. Everything within you protests against you. From the bottom of your feet to the top of your head, nothing's working right… Your country is laid waste, your cities burned down. Your land is destroyed* (or taken over) *by outsiders while you watch, reduced to rubble* (ridicule) *by barbarians"* (1 vs. 2-7 TM) Emphasis mine.

"Oh! Can you believe it? The chaste city has become a whore (or a joke)*! She was once justice, everyone*

living as good neighbors. And now they're all at one another's throats (ethnic tensions). *Your coins are all counterfeits* (devalued currency). *Your wine is watered down* (adulterated value system). *Your leaders are turncoats* (political harlotry and defections) *who keep company with crooks. They sell themselves to the highest bidder* (fat slavery) *and grab anything not nailed down* (cheap policies and principles). *They never stand up for the homeless* (callous and carefree), *never stuck up for the defenseless* (full of injustice)" (vs. 21-23 TM). Emphasis mine.

You can imagine why we are where we are now as a country. I weep for this country overtaken by servants who hold no memories of glory anymore. Yes, I weep, oh, how I weep!

What does God do? The prophet, Isaiah, continues with this verdict from God: *"The Master, God-of-the-Angel-Armies, is emptying Jerusalem (Abuja) and Judah (Nigeria) of all basic necessities, plain bread and water to begin with. He's withdrawing police and protection, judges and courts, pastors and teachers, captains and generals, doctors and nurses, and yes, even the repairmen and jacks-of-all-trades.*

He says, "I'll put little kids (slaves) *in charge of the city. Schoolboys and schoolgirls will order everyone around. People will be at other's throats, stabbing one another in the back: Neighbor against neighbor, young against old, the no-account against the well-respected. One brother will grab another and say, 'You look like you've got a head on your shoulders. Do something! Get us out of this mess! And he'll say, 'Me? Not me! I don't have a clue. Don't put me in charge of anything'. Skinny kids* (suicide bombers, herdsmen) *terrorize my people. Silly girls bully them around. My dear people! Your leaders are taking you down a blind alley. They're sending you off on a wild-goose chase"* (vs. 3:1-7, 12 TM).

Ah, Nigeria! Why are we like this? Our leaders are taking us down the wrong road and what most of us do is stand aside and watch. Corruption and impunity shake hands in our corridors of power and all we do is allow them to divide us and pitch us against one another on the basis of tribe, religion, political party membership, educational background and so on.

Look around, no one seems to have a clue of how to remedy this malady, all we have seen at best is a coalition of the same people – promising much but delivering little. I ask the question again: Where did slaves get the horses they are riding across our lands? How did they manage to topple the real masters and mount the saddle? Was it by rising through the ranks or by revolting against the original just order? If we must address this, the right-thinking ones among us must do the needful now or forever be ruled and ruined by these people.

Back to God of Creation

The Nigeria's anthem, verse two has a clarion call to all of us: 'O God of creation, direct our noble cause…' So, what must we do? First is to go back to our Creator, our God who will overturn and reverse this ugly trend. I have always canvassed for the God-factor to be incorporated into our collective existence as a people. Without the God-factor, nothing makes sense.

Calls for restructuring can only be actualized when we first of all incorporate God Almighty in our scheme of events. He, it is, that will empower us to achieve the much-publicized restructuring of the country. No politician of the present stock has the capacity to put things in order in this country. This is because while some of them are the cabals terrorizing us, others have become hoodwinked and hypnotized by their treachery to either join their bandwagon or be quiet.

We cannot trust the politicians of this age and time because they have largely been the root of our dilemma. Some of them are schooled, no doubt, but sound education which teaches equity, justice and right-living eluded them. The few of them that are thoroughly educated with sound mind have decided to become sleeping giants who are yet awake and report to duty.

Read what God said to His beloved country through His prophet: 'He's withdrawing police and protection, judges and courts', etc. He also says, "I'll put kids in charge of the city. Schoolboys and schoolgirls will order everyone around." Did you see that? They are schooled but not thoroughly educated on quality leadership and good governance. That is why they cannot fix the country. They do not even have a clue due to their poor mind-set. Only people of noble birth and character can fix this country and get us out.

Proverbs 28:2 says, *"When the country is in chaos, everybody has a plan to fix it – but it takes a leaders of real understanding* (not presumed understanding) *to straighten things out"* (TM.) Emphasis mine.

President Solomon was on point with this salient truth even as it has been playing out in the country. Since the advent of democracy, nay, back from independence in 1960, men of different ideologies have, at one time tried their 'best'. But instead of fixing it, they fix themselves, their families, their cronies and buddies and left the land to lay waste. They never left us better than they met us.

Even in this era of change by the current ruling political party, the groaning of Nigerians, the brain drain, insecurity by terrorizing herdsmen and kidnappers appeared to have doubled in couple of years. Yet, they once promised to banish terrorism and their sponsors into oblivion, turn their hideouts including Sambisa forest into museums and recreation parks, fix the worsening electric power situation like 'a sensible government should do in six months', and provide basic amenities to all and sundry irrespective of ethnic background or religious affiliations. How far have they fared after

two years? Same guards, same story! They cannot fool God even though they can fool men. More so, they cannot fool all men all the time.

God says that He is withdrawing essential services and putting kids in charge. So, what can we do about that? Already we have "children" in positions of influence. Woe to the land whose king is a child! Do you see the correlation? President Solomon saw it happen. Prophet Isaiah saw it coming. Now, we are witnessing it in our time and land. Too bad!

Look at the terrorism in the North East, according to the Prophet: *"Skinny kids terrorize my people" and "Silly girls bully them around"* (3:12 TM). Who are the ones being used by Boko Haram – skinny and hungry kids, and silly but homeless girls who blow themselves up in mosques and churches, killing people anyhow. These are poor children of the poor who successive leadership and regimes controlled by cabals neglected and abandoned, but have become a source of terror to the land and her people. If they had been adequately cared for – educated, trained in skills and vocations, empowered to make a difference in their generation like their counterparts in Europe, America, Asia and Australia, we would not have these negative indices in our records.

Unfortunately, that is the case because those privileged to mount the throne have betrayed their divine mandate by refusing to provide serene environment for those "skinny" kids and "silly" girls to become strong and sound children we should be proud of. Soon and very soon, the table shall be turned, and the original inheritors and heirs to the throne will take over. I optimistically look to that day.

On a final note, Nigerians and indeed all Africans must begin to come together as one united front to confront these men of error in power at any level. Yes, we must, within the ambient of the law, begin to confront them with the truth of the hopelessness that is written all over the faces of the common man, and equally demand that they step down, step aside or step out, and that, forever. This is so that we can be free again.

Second, the nobles and those with noble character should begin to form strong coalitions in order to dismantle the unholy, lopsided and unfair arrangement where slaves rule and princes rue in our land. Until good men arise and take the front line in this fight to restructure the system, slaves would continue to hold sway. Until men of noble birth, blood and behavior get out of their comfort zones to pursue the just cause of setting things right for the benefit and blessing of all – the future in view, the slaves in power would continue to hold this land to ransom, to ridicule, and in the doldrums. Now is the time to react. And until we react, even Heaven will not act!